Luis Troyano
BAKE IT GREAT

PAVILION

For Louise, my very patient and loving wife (and chief taster).

A special thank you also to my small army of testers and taste advisers: Mum, Craig, Janine, Zara, Amy, Katie, Rita, Roy, Wendy and Barry.

Annie, Emily and the team at Pavilion: thank you for making my publishing dream come true.

Luis Troyano

BAKE IT GREAT

Contents

Introduction

I absolutely love baking. It's a creative outlet that also gives you something to eat.

But, for me, it's not just about the baking. I think it's true that you really do eat with your eyes first. When you are in a bakery, cake shop, supermarket, or just flicking through a recipe book looking for a tasty treat, your eyes make the first decision, closely followed by taste preferences. Secondly, bakers enjoy giving. My baking obsession allows me to do just that. The feeling when I reveal a bake to my family and friends simply can't be beaten. I want it to look great and create a wow factor. Equally it must taste good, and provide a memory that lasts. Bakes make the perfect gift.

I want to show you how easy it is to bake. This book eliminates guessing when bakes are ready to come out of the oven. And every recipe has been chosen to show there's no need for a vast amount of equipment or shop-bought decorations.

I'm on a mission to demystify baking science, finishing and decoration. Whether it's a simple loaf or a complex layered cake, let's make it look fabulous. I'll show you techniques that can take a bake from everyday to showstopping. But ultimately I hope you'll let your creative juices flow and put your own stamp on your baking.

About me

I'm a graphic designer, beekeeper and baking obsessive. 2014 was an amazing year; I was fortunate enough to be a finalist on series five of *The Great British Bake Off*. I became known for my designs and being different. To be honest, though, I just baked my way through, had a ball and made a really great new group of friends.

My parents moved to the UK from Spain in the 1960s. Being brought up in a Spanish household meant food has always played an important part in my life. My father was a waiter in restaurants. At about the age of twelve, to earn pocket money, I worked in the restaurant after school. My job was to wash the glasses. I eventually progressed to working behind the bar and waiting on people; it was a thorough grounding, and in combination with my Spanish background gave me the passionate love of food I have now. I'm a self-taught cook, and

about seven years ago I realized I was in awe of bakers who could create wonderful baked things. It was something I had never explored. So I set out on my baking journey with a mission to figure out the mysteries of how flour can be transformed in so many ways.

Thinking about it, I'm constantly blown away by how many things can be made from four basic ingredients: flour, eggs, sugar and butter. Combine that with the pleasure I get from baking for family and friends, and life doesn't get any better. Baking is a relaxing pastime that should allow the baker to be creative and forget any worries. It's probably the little boy in me that enjoys the chemistry part of mixing all the ingredients together and seeing what happens. The artist in me enjoys perfecting the look and decoration of a bake.

Never fail basics

MY BAKING ETHOS

It's pretty simple really: leave nothing to chance. And that's exactly what I've done when writing this book. I've made no assumptions about the reader's knowledge. There's no abbreviated recipe speak; everything is explained in detail. I don't like bakes failing, so why should I expect it to happen to anyone else? Baking takes time, and it's important that it's right first time.

I've tried to organize each chapter in terms of techniques, starting with recipes that are very achievable. Read the recipe through first and always take your time when baking, it really makes a difference to the end result. People eat with their eyes first, so presentation is important, too. Let's be honest, we all like praise and want to be told how fabulous something looks when it is brought out and presented to family and friends.

TIMINGS

Be realistic when you want to bake something. Pick a recipe that is achievable in the time you have. I have put an estimated time on every recipe to help you decide. Don't forget, though, that a lot of bakes can be done in stages to fit around your own schedule. Bread can be made over a couple of days (see pages 28–30), cake sponges and fillings made the day before you assemble them. You don't need to spend a straight three or four hours in the kitchen.

INGREDIENTS

There's nothing too fancy in this book. A pet hate of mine is trawling the shops trying to find that elusive ingredient that is only in stock three times a year. Every recipe in this book uses off-the-shelf ingredients. Where something is a little more specialist, I have suggested an alternative. Admittedly some ingredients are far easier sourced online, such as aniseeds or glacé fruits; I buy a couple of packs at a time and they last ages.

Don't get hung up about making everything yourself. I frequently use bought pastry, jams, curds, spreads, etc. Baking should be enjoyable and not a chore.

Most of the flours I use are nothing out of the ordinary, but when I need to roll out any type of bread dough I use rice flour to dust the work surface. It has excellent non-stick properties as well as being flavourless. I buy it at my local Indian supermarket – much better value than the big supermarkets.

When it comes to yeast, I always use instant. Readily available and totally reliable, I don't see the need to use any other form.

There's a huge array of blocks of butter available in the shops. I keep it simple – just buy basic unsalted. This gives you the control of adding your own salt to taste. All the recipes in this book are written to that principle.

Make sure you stick to the egg sizes given in recipes, as this can make a huge difference to the outcome of a bake. I only use two sizes: medium and large.

When I want to add a vanilla flavour to a bake, I tend to use vanilla paste rather than extract. It will give you a much better flavour.

Finally, always use food colouring gels rather than liquids. Not only do you need much less colouring, you also don't dilute the bake mixture and get a much more vibrant colour.

EQUIPMENT

Baking (and cooking in general) should be accessible to everyone. I'm a firm believer in that. So to that end, I've tried to limit the amount of equipment required to make the recipes in this book.

When coming up with the recipes, I went through my kitchen and picked my most-used tins. There's nothing more frustrating than picking up a recipe and thinking 'yes, I'm going to make that', only to find you need a specialist tin that takes two weeks to arrive. With one or two exceptions, such as the angel food cake tin, all the tins in this book are easily available at your local supermarket or are commonly stocked at online retailers. I've kept the selection to a minimum, meaning you get to use them again and again.

Every recipe in this book lists the key equipment that you will need to make it. I've included detailed sizes of tins, cases, cutters – everything I can think of to take away any risk of failure – so if you are shopping for tins, you can buy identical products.

If you really enjoy baking, there are some pieces of equipment I would recommend you invest in. Firstly, a good kitchen mixer with a paddle, dough hook and whisk is probably the best purchase you will make. It will make life easy and let you zoom through the preparation of a bake. I'm as lazy as the next person and use my mixer pretty much all the time for kneading dough, whipping cream, beating cake mixes, in fact anything I think I can put into it without destroying it. If you don't want to go to the expense of a stand mixer at first, a good electric hand mixer will get you going.

A good food processor is probably the next best thing to buy. It will quickly blitz, blend, whisk and crumb for you. Making pastry becomes a breeze.

Oven gloves. I don't mean to state the obvious, but there's oven gloves and there's oven gloves. Invest in a pair with fingers, it will pretty much change your life!

Scales are important. They should be large enough to pop a bowl on and still be able to see the display. Success in baking comes from accurate weighing. You'll also need a good set of measuring spoons.

Silicone-coated non-stick baking parchment. This is one of the most common points of failure in baking. You've spent hours creating that masterpiece and it's welded itself to the tin. Seriously – forget greaseproof paper and cheap parchments. Buy good-quality silicone-coated non-stick baking parchment and use it all the time.

A temperature probe with a digital read-out; I use a Thermapen, and not just for baking, but for other types of cooking, too. But for testing when a cake is done, I use a thin metal skewer (see page 13).

A couple of baking sheets; I use aluminium sheets that measure 38 x 32cm – a couple of sturdy ones will last a lifetime; don't buy cheap, thin ones that warp when they get hot and wobble as you take them out of the oven. You'll also need a large wire cooling rack.

Other than that, different sized bowls, large and small balloon whisks, a heatproof measuring jug, rolling pin, rubber spatulas, a palette knife, a sieve, pastry brush, a set of piping nozzles from 1mm to 12mm, and you are pretty much done. I always use disposable piping bags: I can't be doing with the washing up. Oh, and I couldn't live without my bench scraper – because it's the quickest way of cleaning the worktop no matter what I'm baking.

OVEN SETTINGS, TEMPERATURES & POSITIONING

I find it unbelievable and frustrating that most recipe books don't talk about this. It makes a huge difference to the outcome of anything that is baked. Every recipe in this book has a recommended setting and position of where to place it in the oven. The position refers to the bake, not the shelf. So imagine the centre line of the cake tin, loaf, whatever the bake is, and that's what the oven position refers to. Breads always bake better in the centre of an oven with the fan off; they prefer hot still air. Cakes, on the other hand, are best baked with the fan on, and in the lower half of the oven. I bake cakes on the bottom shelf most of the time. This keeps them out of the way of strong fans and high heat, and stops them from drying out too quickly; the cake rises evenly and the top stays nice and flat.

Firstly, always take time to preheat your oven to the required temperature for at least 15 minutes. Where you place something on a shelf is really important too when using a fan oven. You are probably familiar with your oven and realize there's always a particular corner where things brown too quickly. This is because oven fans tend to blow air around in a circular direction. The start of this circle is the hottest, hence your oven hot spot. The key to success is not to place items on the centre of a shelf, but rather to one side, away from the hot spot. You will be amazed at the difference this will make to your bakes.

If I have more than one tray of items I need to put in the oven, I will generally bake them separately. Placing two trays of bread rolls in the oven at the same time but on different shelves will inevitably end up with one batch being baked before the other and inconsistent results. I do bake tins of cake sponges at the same time, but where they won't fit on one shelf, I place the higher tin to one side, out of the hot spot, and the lower tin at the opposite side, below the hot spot.

I'm a great advocate of baking stones. That sounds expensive, but it needn't be. Buy a cheap stone cutting board from your local supermarket and remove the rubber feet. Placed on the shelf in the preheating oven it will store the heat and give you the most amazing results, especially when baking bread. It's the nearest you will get to a professional bakery oven in your home.

Note: the oven temperatures in degrees Fahrenheit (°F) are based on the fan setting, as fan ovens are now more common than any other type. I have included non-fan temperatures in degrees Celsius (°C) because this is the best way to cook bread and other yeast doughs, but do check each recipe for recommended oven settings.

Oven shelf positions

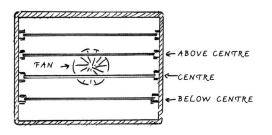

Multiple tin positions using fan

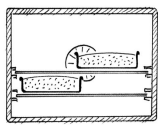

Fan hot spot

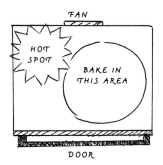

WHEN ARE BAKES READY?

Here's my secret to making great bakes: knowing when something is ready to come out of the oven. How many times have you read 'look for the wobble in the centre' and 'tap the bottom and listen if it sounds hollow'? I'm sure those techniques work sometimes, but how much wobble, what's the right hollow sound? So let's forget that. Most bakes are ready when they reach an optimum internal temperature. No matter what, if that particular temperature has been hit then rest assured it's baked to perfection. This is particularly useful knowledge when making custard-based bakes and breads. Reach the optimum temperature and the crumb of your bread will be light and airy.

The most common mistake made when making custard tarts is over-baking them. Eggs set at a certain temperature, so once the centre of the tart reaches that temperature it must set, no matter how unbaked it may look. Custard tarts continue to set as they cool. So test the centre of the tart with an accurate temperature probe and when it just hits 75°C/167°F, take it out of the oven. It should still have quite a wobble but when cool you will have the most amazing custard tart, baked to perfection.

So the one key piece of equipment I would encourage you to buy is a good temperature probe with a digital display. I use a Thermapen because it's quick to respond, thin and needle-like, and very sensitive. Always take a reading from the centre of the bake.

But when it comes to cakes, the old-fashioned skewer test is always reliable. Insert a thin metal skewer into the centre of the cake; if it comes out clean, the cake is ready. It's really important that the skewer comes out completely clean before you take the cake out of the oven or it will sink in the middle as it cools and be soggy.

Also look for the cake just coming away from the side of the tin. If you touch the centre gently, it should feel just firm.

Never open the oven door until you are in the last quarter of the total baking time, or your sponge will deflate. Invest in a good pair of oven gloves and always test cakes while they are still in the oven: don't take them out; carefully reach in to test and then, if the cake is not ready, close the oven door.

Here are the optimum temperatures to look for:

Egg custard-based bakes: 75°C/167°F

Bread: 90°C/195°F

Cake: 99°C/210°F

It's also useful to take a temperature reading when cooking raw meats and fish:

Fish: 60°C/140°F

Chicken: 74°C/165°F

Pork: 75°C/167°F

Beef: rare 52°C/126°F
medium 60°C/140°F
well done 71°C/160°F

Lamb: rare 52°C/126°F
medium 60°C/140°F
well done 71°C/160°F

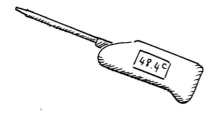

MEASURING & WEIGHING

I can't stress how important this is. Baking does have a scientific element to it, so always use good, accurate scales and measuring spoons. Where a measurement is given in a spoon size, it means a level spoonful: 1 teaspoon = 5ml and 1 tablespoon = 15ml. Don't try to guess or the bakes won't be quite right – or worse, they may fail.

I tend to write the weights of bowls and tins in permanent marker on the underside of them. You wouldn't believe how useful that is when you need to know the weight of an ingredient or mixture. Just weigh the whole thing and deduct the weight of the holding item.

To get even layers for cakes, I always put the same quantity of mixture into each tin. The simplest way to do this is to weigh the empty mixer bowl that you will make the sponge mix in. To find out how much mix you have, weigh the full bowl and subtract the weight of the empty bowl. Place the cake tins on your scales and weigh the mixture going into each one.

GREASING & LINING TINS FOR EASY RELEASE OF BAKES

I never leave anything to chance. It really is worth spending 5 minutes to grease and line a tin well. Easy removal of the cake or loaf is guaranteed.

For greasing, there are some great cooking mists and sprays available that make the job very easy. Simply give the inside of the tin a quick spray all over. To line the tin, always use silicone-coated non-stick baking parchment. Very little sticks to it. Line the bottom of the tin first, followed by the sides. Use the grease to stick the parchment to the tin.

When lining the bottom of tins with a round piece of non-stick baking parchment, draw around the loose bottom as a guide. Leave a tab of parchment on the side of the circle – this will give you something to hold as you slide bakes from the parchment.

When working with tin shapes that don't lend themselves to lining with parchment, such as bundt tins, use a pastry brush to give the tin a really thorough, even coating of soft unsalted butter. Then throw in a handful of plain flour or ground almonds and move the tin around to coat the inside completely. Tip the tin upside down and knock out any excess. You will also be able to spot if you missed any bits.

When the bake has come out of the oven, leave it to cool in the tin for 10 minutes before attempting to remove it. This cooling period lets the bake contract, firm up and release from the sides of the tin.

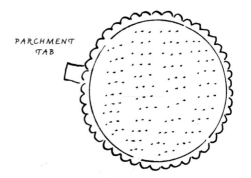

PARCHMENT TAB

Shortcrust pastry

There's absolutely no need to fear making and using pastry. However, the first few times you make a tart, I would recommend using ready-made pastry. Doing that lets you get a feel for working with pastry before attempting your own.

Here are the four kinds of pastry I use the most. To be honest, the first and second ones are my go-to pastries for pretty much everything. Both are robust and at the same time have a really crisp flaked finish when baked. Once you start adding chocolate and almonds the pastry becomes slightly harder to work with.

I always make my pastry using a food processor. The less you handle it, the better, and it's also a lot quicker than making it by hand. However, you can rub the butter and dry ingredients together using your fingertips in the traditional way.

The quantities below make enough pastry to line a tart tin up to 28cm in diameter. You can make the pastry and keep it in the fridge for up to 2 days before using it. However, always take it out of the fridge and let it come to room temperature for about 40 minutes before trying to roll it.

MAKES ENOUGH TO LINE A 28CM TART TIN

Time required: 15 minutes, if using a food processor

INGREDIENTS

Shortcrust pastry
250g plain flour
½ tsp fine salt
150g cold unsalted butter, cut into 1cm cubes
1 medium egg
1 tbsp fridge-cold water

Sweet shortcrust pastry
215g plain flour
30g icing sugar
120g cold unsalted butter, cut into 1cm cubes
2 medium egg yolks
2 tbsp fridge-cold water

Chocolate shortcrust pastry
250g plain flour
30g unsweetened cocoa powder
90g caster sugar
½ tsp fine salt
140g cold unsalted butter, cut into 1cm cubes
1 medium egg
2 tbsp fridge-cold water

Chocolate and almond shortcrust pastry
220g plain flour
40g golden caster sugar
40g ground almonds
3 tbsp unsweetened cocoa powder
½ tsp fine salt
150g cold unsalted butter, cut into 1cm cubes
2 medium egg yolks
2 tbsp fridge-cold water

METHOD
The method is the same for all four kinds of pastry.

Place all the dry ingredients in the bowl of your food processor and give them a quick pulse.

Add the butter and pulse until the mixture resembles breadcrumbs.

Tip the mixture into a large mixing bowl and add the egg and water.

Bring together with your hands and then gently knead the mixture a couple of times to make a smooth pastry.

Wrap in clingfilm and place in the fridge until required.

Lining tart tins & blind baking

Use tart tins with loose bottoms. Always grease the tin before lining it. Line the bottom of the tin with a round piece of non-stick baking parchment, drawing around the loose bottom as a guide. Leave a tab of parchment on the side of the circle – this will give you something to hold as you slide the tart from the parchment.

Forget baking parchment and ceramic beans for blind baking; use a good-quality clingfilm and rice or mung beans instead. The clingfilm won't melt in the oven and the rice or mung beans get into every nook and cranny. The clingfilm is non-stick too; you can just lift it out after blind baking with the rice or beans.

Time required: 45 minutes, plus cooling time
Optimum oven position and setting: centre and fan

METHOD

Preheat the oven to 190°C fan/210°C/ 375°F/gas 6½. Grease and line the bottom of the tart tin (see above) and place it on a baking sheet. If the pastry has been in the fridge, take it out and let it come to room temperature for 30–45 minutes before attempting to roll it.

Flour your work surface lightly but evenly with plain flour. Roll out the pastry to a thickness of 3mm. Keep lifting and rotating the pastry to stop it sticking to your work surface. Use more flour as required. I sprinkle some on the pastry and rub it across the surface to keep it non-stick. Place your tin gently on the pastry and cut around it, about 6cm larger than the tin.

Sprinkle the surface of the pastry with a little flour and rub it in gently with your hand. Fold the pastry over on itself twice so you end up with a quarter wedge. Place the point of the wedge in the centre of the tin and simply unfold it. Keep an offcut of pastry on one side.

Gently ease the pastry into the sides of the tin. Dip the offcut of pastry in flour and use it to gently press the pastry into the sides of the tin. Do not trim off the overhanging pastry. Prick the base of the pastry all over with a fork.

Place four sheets of clingfilm loosely over the tart tin, and press them down together into the pastry. Gather the excess clingfilm around the tin. Fill the tin with rice or mung beans and bake for 20 minutes.

Remove from the oven and leave to cool for 5 minutes.

Gently lift out the clingfilm with the rice or beans and put them into a large bowl to cool before you store them.

Put the pastry back in the oven and bake for 8 minutes until it looks dry and pale golden. Sometimes the pastry base will inflate during this phase of baking. If you see this happening, open the oven and prick the base with a toothpick to let the air escape. Plug that hole with a small ball of raw pastry as soon as the pastry comes out of the oven.

Remove from the oven and leave to cool for 20 minutes. Trim off the excess pastry by running a sharp, smooth knife around the top of the tin.

TIP *Repairing a blind-baked pastry case*

If you think you may have a slight crack or hole in your blind-baked pastry case, here's a quick and easy way of repairing it just after it has come out of the oven. Brush a thick layer of beaten egg over the hole or crack. Place the case back in the oven for a couple of minutes and the egg will set, sealing the potential leak. Repeat if necessary.

TIP *Sealing a pastry case*

Tarts with a wet filling require a sealed pastry case. If left for too long before serving, the pastry will go soggy. The simplest and quickest way to prevent this is to brush the inside of the pastry case with beaten egg after blind baking and pop it back in the oven for a minute to dry it off.

If the pastry case is not being baked again, a tasty way to seal it is to brush the inside with melted chocolate (about 100g) and leave it to set. It takes a little time but adds another flavour dimension to the tart.

Hot water crust pastry

This is a never-fail recipe for hot water crust pastry that will crisp up beautifully during baking and has a wonderful short texture. Try adding some dried herbs or spices to the pastry mix, you will be amazed with the results. You can also colour the pastry, using ½ teaspoon of turmeric for a vibrant yellow, or beetroot powder for a deep red.

METHOD

Place the flours, salt and pepper in a large mixing bowl.

Place the butter, lard and water in a small saucepan and bring to the boil. Allow to cool slightly, then pour onto the flour mixture and stir with a large wooden spoon.

After a minute or so, it should have cooled enough for you to get your hands in and bring the mixture together into a dough. Tip it out onto a clean surface and knead it for a minute or so until you have a smooth, elastic pastry.

As a general rule of thumb, use two-thirds of the pastry to line the tin and the remaining third for the lid and decorations.

Grease your chosen tin with a little butter or lard before lining.

MAKES ENOUGH PASTRY TO LINE ONE OF THE FOLLOWING TINS AND LEAVE ENOUGH LEFT OVER TO MAKE SOME PASTRY DECORATIONS

900g/2lb loaf tin
(the base of mine measures 95 x 195mm and the tin is 70mm high)
OR
23cm non-stick springform cake tin

Time required: 20 minutes

INGREDIENTS

400g plain flour
150g strong white bread flour
½ tsp fine salt
½ tsp ground black pepper
80g unsalted butter
100g lard
200ml water

Cheat's puff pastry

OK, so technically this is a rough puff pastry, but it's not far off a full-on puff pastry in texture when baked. It's perfect for a wide variety of applications, from topping pies, making pasties and parcels, sausage rolls or sweet slices.

This is really quick and easy, but you will need a food processor fitted with a blade to make it. You can make the pastry and keep it in the fridge for up to 2 days before using it.

Time required:
30 minutes, plus chilling

INGREDIENTS
250g plain flour
½ tsp fine salt
250g fridge-cold unsalted butter
2 tsp lemon juice
110ml ice-cold water

METHOD
Place the flour and salt in the bowl of your food processor and give them a quick pulse.

Take 200g of the cold butter and cut it into 5mm slices. Add them to the food processor and pulse a few times to combine, but don't overdo it – you want big chunks of butter visible. Place the remaining butter in the freezer.

Tip the flour and butter mixture into a large bowl and work in the lemon juice and water, using a table knife. Don't handle the mixture at this stage. Tip it out onto your work surface and shape it into a ball. Wrap it in clingfilm and place it in the fridge for 45 minutes to firm up the butter.

Take it out and roll it out to a rectangle approximately 35 x 12cm, with a short side nearest you.

Using a coarse grater, grate the frozen butter over the rectangle.

Fold the top third of the pastry down and the bottom third up over it. Turn the dough 90 degrees, and repeat the rolling and folding process twice more. Wrap the pastry in clingfilm and place it back in the fridge for a minimum of 45 minutes before using it.

Custards

In my world there are two distinct types of custard: the one that sets as soon as it cools and is reminiscent of school dinners, and the much more delicate, pourable crème anglaise.

Here are both versions. If you are making a trifle or just want a good old-fashioned custard to go with a sponge pudding, then make the thick version. Let the custard cool before pouring it into a trifle and then let it set in the fridge, preferably overnight.

The crème anglaise is a much thinner sauce, perfect for pretty much any dessert. It's a great base for the French classic dessert of floating islands.

Time required: 20 minutes

INGREDIENTS

Thick custard
400ml whole milk
100ml double cream
4 large egg yolks
120g caster sugar
1 tsp vanilla paste
2 tbsp cornflour

**Thin pouring custard
(crème anglaise)**
250ml whole milk
100ml double cream
4 large egg yolks
85g caster sugar
1½ tsp vanilla paste

METHOD

Both custards are made the same way.

Put the milk and cream in a large saucepan over a low heat and bring to just below boiling point.

In a large heatproof bowl, whisk together the egg yolks, sugar and vanilla until smooth and pale. If making the thick custard, whisk in the cornflour until well combined. Pour the hot milk into the egg mixture in a slow steady stream, whisking all the time.

Put the mixture back in the saucepan over a low heat, stirring all the time until it thickens and coats the back of a spoon. You can cook it to perfection by using a temperature probe: the custard is ready when it reaches 75°C/167°F. Be careful not to take it much higher than 80°C/176°F or it will curdle.

Crème pâtissière

Also known as pastry cream or crème pat, crème pâtissière is an extremely versatile ingredient for cakes and pastries. Cold, it can be used as a filling, whipped and even baked. Hot, it can be poured into a blind-baked pastry case as the basis for a French fruit tart. I always make it the day before I need it and keep it in the fridge overnight.

Time required: 20 minutes

INGREDIENTS

Vanilla crème pâtissière
Approx. 500g
(Used in the Brioche twists on page 97)
350ml whole milk
1 medium egg
2 medium egg yolks
45g caster sugar
45g cornflour
1 tsp vanilla paste

Vanilla crème pâtissière
Approx. 900g
700ml whole milk
1 medium egg
5 medium egg yolks
85g caster sugar
75g cornflour
2 tsp vanilla paste

Chocolate crème pâtissière
Approx. 500g
(Used in the Chocolate and salted caramel swirls on page 176)
280ml whole milk
4 large egg yolks
50g caster sugar
25g cornflour
25g unsweetened cocoa
   powder
25g dark chocolate

Chocolate crème pâtissière
Approx. 900g
(Used in the Chocolate and amaretto prinsesstårta on page 57 and the Chocolate heaven profiteroles on page 193)
500ml whole milk
7 large egg yolks
100g caster sugar
40g cornflour
40g unsweetened cocoa
   powder
50g dark chocolate

Peanut butter crème pâtissière
Approx. 1kg
(Used in the Peanut butter and chocolate doughnuts on page 104)
600ml whole milk
100ml double cream
1 medium egg
5 medium egg yolks
85g caster sugar
75g cornflour
2 tsp vanilla paste
200g smooth peanut butter

METHOD

The method is the same for all four kinds of crème pâtissière.

Pour the milk into a large saucepan.

Place the eggs and sugar in a large heatproof bowl and whisk until pale and fluffy. Then whisk in the cornflour and vanilla paste or cocoa, if using.

Heat the milk until just boiling. Pour slowly into the egg mixture while whisking all the time with a balloon whisk until well mixed and smooth.

Return the mixture to the saucepan over a medium heat (add the dark chocolate here if making the chocolate flavour) and whisk continuously for 3 minutes while the mixture bubbles.

Pour back into the heatproof bowl (whisk in the peanut butter until smooth if making the peanut butter flavour).

Cover with clingfilm, making sure the clingfilm is actually touching the surface of the crème pâtissière to prevent a skin forming.

Whipped cream & buttercream

I am often asked how I get my whipped cream so thick and stable that it supports heavy layers and decorations, yet it is still totally smooth.

The secret is to use double cream and add icing sugar, which stabilizes the cream and gives it strength. It's excellent for piping as it holds its shape and doesn't melt. When making a flavoured whipped cream, always add your flavouring after whipping the cream to soft peaks. This builds air and stability in the mix and then you generally just need a quick last whisk to get it to stiff peaks. Never over-whip cream: you want it just to the stiff peaks stage. Manipulating cream – for example, placing it in a piping bag or spreading it – makes it thicken, so not over-whipping compensates for that.

WHIPPED CREAM

Here is the formula I work to:

For every 100ml double cream, add 1 tbsp icing sugar.

For vanilla-flavoured cream, add ¼ tsp vanilla paste for every 100ml cream.

If you are adding liqueur for flavour, add 1 tbsp for every 100ml cream.

TIP *Making butter*

Did you know you can make the most delicious butter with cream? If I have a tub of cream in the fridge and its best before date is approaching, I just pop it in a mixer and whisk until it separates and butter is formed. Take it out of the mixer, shape it and give it a quick rinse in clean water. You can flavour it with salt, garlic or herbs, then freeze it for future use. Rolled and wrapped in parchment it makes the most amazing gift.

BUTTERCREAM

I find using a kitchen mixer fitted with a whisk makes the best buttercream. The machine has the power to whip it really well and get it super smooth and light. There's nothing worse than a grainy buttercream in my opinion.

Use soft unsalted butter and whisk in the icing sugar first. I leave it whisking for a good 5 minutes at high speed, scraping down the bowl regularly. When smooth and creamy, add the milk and any flavouring you are using, such as vanilla paste, zests or essences.

Here is the formula I work to:

For every 250g soft unsalted butter, add 750g icing sugar and 3 tbsp milk.

For vanilla-flavoured buttercream, add 2 tsp vanilla paste for every 250g unsalted butter.

If you are adding liqueur for flavour, add 2 tbsp for every 250g unsalted butter.

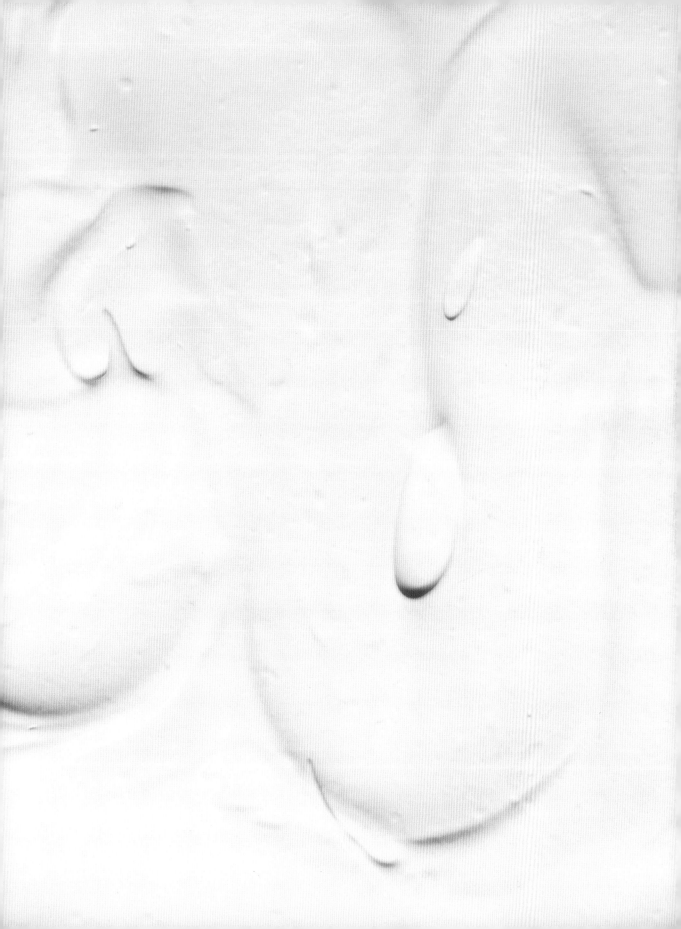

How to make jam

Making jam is incredibly easy and a great way to use up and preserve leftover fruit. You don't need any fancy equipment, but a temperature probe or sugar/jam thermometer is useful. Jam sugar contains pectin, a gelling agent, to help the jam to set.

Sterile jars are the key to keeping homemade jam long term. Give the jars a really good wash in hot soapy water or a dishwasher and place them in the preheated oven while you make the jam. I would always recommend you use new lids: put the lids into a pan of boiling water for 5 minutes, then place them on a clean towel to dry.

Time required: 45 minutes

INGREDIENTS
soft fruits
jam sugar – the same weight
    as the soft fruits
2 tbsp lemon juice
10g unsalted butter

METHOD
Preheat the oven to 100°C fan/120°C/210°F/gas ¼. Put the jam jars in the oven. Place a small plate in the freezer.

Wash your fruits in fresh water, then weigh them, making a note of the weight. If you want smooth jam, purée the fruits in a food processor. Place them in a large pan. If using one, clip your jam thermometer to the side of the pan with the end in the fruit.

Add the same weight of jam sugar to the pan and warm gently over a medium heat, stirring all the time, until the sugar has dissolved.

Add the lemon juice and butter. Increase the heat to high and bring the mixture to a rolling boil. For jam to set, the mixture needs to be brought to 105°C/220°F. Keep an eye on your jam thermometer and when it reaches the target temperature, turn off the heat. If you don't have a thermometer, boil for 5 minutes.

Take the small plate from the freezer. Drizzle a teaspoon of the jam onto it. Place in the fridge for a couple of minutes. The jam on the plate should form a skin, which will crinkle when pushed with your finger. If it is still runny, bring the jam to a rolling boil for another 3–4 minutes and retest.

Take the jars out of the oven and leave the jam to cool in the pan for 10 minutes. This will help the jam to set.

Pour the jam into the jars to within 5mm of the top and immediately screw on the lids. As the jam cools a vacuum will form.

If you want to use the jam immediately, pour it into a large roasting tin to allow it to cool and set quickly.

Perfect lemon curd

Homemade lemon curd is a delicious treat on toast or scones, or you can mix it with whipped cream and use it to fill a sponge sandwich cake or éclairs (page 186). You will need a temperature probe and a large jar and lid (put the lid into a pan of boiling water for 5 minutes, then drain on a clean towel).

MAKES ABOUT 350G

Time required: 45 minutes

INGREDIENTS

100ml lemon juice, strained
finely grated zest of
   3 unwaxed lemons
75g soft unsalted butter
225g caster sugar
3 large eggs
1 tbsp cornflour

METHOD

Preheat the oven to 120°C fan/140°C/ 250°F/gas 1. Give the jar a good wash and place it in the oven to sterilize it.

Place all the ingredients in a medium saucepan. Using an electric hand whisk, give it all a good mix up for a minute. It will look split and curdled, but don't worry!

Take the jar out of the oven and set aside to cool slightly.

Insert a temperature probe in the curd mixture. Place the saucepan over a low heat and stir continuously. As the mixture warms, it will become smooth and glossy and will start to thicken. Once the temperature reaches 78°C/172°F it's cooked to perfection; it will set as it cools.

Pour it into the jar and immediately seal with the lid. Leave to cool and then place in the fridge, where it will last for up to 7 days.

Kneading dough & your first loaf of bread

I can wax lyrical for hours on why everyone should try making a loaf of bread. It really is so satisfying, and the result is totally delicious. So here is the perfect beginners' loaf of white bread. This is the starting point for the bread journey you are about to embark on; trust me, you will be making more. Use your hands to make and knead your first loaf to get a feel for the dough.

The best environment in which to bake bread is still and hot, so when baking bread I always recommend *not* using a fan oven. I find it a little too harsh, over-baking the outside of the loaf before the inside is baked. If you don't have the option of baking without a fan, just place the loaf lower in the oven.

A good temperature probe is essential for the perfect loaf. The inside centre of a loaf is cooked to perfection when it reaches 90°C/195°F. The temperature probe inserted into the centre takes away the guesswork.

MAKES 1 LOAF

Time required: 20 minutes preparation and two proves

Baking time:
30–40 minutes

Optimum oven position and setting: centre and no fan, with a baking stone (see tip)

Essential equipment:
A 900g/2lb loaf tin; the base of mine measures 95 x 195mm and the tin is 70mm high. Grease and line it with non-stick baking parchment
You will also need a large plastic bag to put the tin into for proving

INGREDIENTS

500g strong white bread flour, plus extra for dusting
10g instant yeast
1 tsp fine salt
320ml cool water
a little rapeseed oil for greasing the proving bowl

METHOD

Put the flour, yeast and salt in a large mixing bowl. When adding the yeast and salt, place them at opposite sides of the bowl.

Add 300ml of the water and begin to mix it all together with your fingers. Work it really well to pick up all the dry ingredients, creating a sticky dough. Add a little more water if required. At this stage it's quite messy, but the kneading will change the consistency.

Kneading the dough activates the gluten in the flour, making the dough smooth and elastic. Hold one end of the dough with one hand and push the dough away from you with the palm of the other. Roll the dough back on itself and repeat for about 10 minutes. I don't flour the work surface while doing this as it changes the composition of the dough. Just persevere and the dough will come together; your hands should be clean by the end of the kneading process.

There are a few ways of telling when the dough is kneaded perfectly. It should be just tacky with a smooth skin and not sticking to your hands. You should be able to stretch it about 20cm without it tearing. If you hold it up to a window and pull it gently, you should be able to get it thin enough to see the light through it, which is known as the windowpane test.

continues overleaf...

Lightly oil a large bowl and place the dough in it. Cover it with clingfilm or a shower cap and set it aside until doubled in size. You don't need to leave it somewhere warm – it will prove quite happily at a cool room temperature. Depending on your room temperature this can take 1 hour, but it's fine to leave it for 2 hours.

Next, knock back the dough. This is the process of getting rid of the air the yeast has created. It makes the texture of the final loaf uniform as well as making it easier to handle when shaping. Tip the dough out onto a lightly floured surface – I use rice flour (see tip). Fold the dough over on itself until all the air has been knocked out of it.

Pull the dough into a rough rectangle a little wider than the loaf tin and about 30cm long. Fold one third of the dough over into the centre, and then the remaining third over that one. Tuck the two ends under and place the dough in the tin. Place in a bag to prove or just pop a shower cap over the tin. This stops the skin of the dough drying out. Set aside to prove again for 45–60 minutes until doubled in size. The dough should have risen just above the rim of the loaf tin.

While the loaf proves, preheat the oven to 200°C fan/ 220°C/390°F/gas 7.

When the loaf has risen, dust the top with a little flour, using a fine sieve. Bake for 30–40 minutes.

When ready, it should have a deep golden colour and sound hollow when tapped. You can test if it is baked to perfection by using a temperature probe: the centre of the loaf should be just over 90°C/195°F. Place on a wire rack to cool for about 30 minutes before slicing.

TIPS

Baking stone
A baking stone is an excellent buy. This sounds fancy, but it isn't. Just get a cheap granite cutting board (about 40 x 30cm) from your local supermarket and remove the rubber feet. Place this on the shelf in the oven when preheating and it will store heat and cook your bread from the bottom, giving your loaf a perfectly baked crisp base.

Rice flour for rolling out dough
When I need to roll out any type of bread dough, I use rice flour to dust the surface. It's completely non-stick as well as flavourless.

Don't let dough run your life
There is a popular misconception that bread takes all day to make and requires constant attention. It really doesn't. Use your fridge and freezer to manage dough and make the yeast work around your lifestyle.

Dough can be made the night before and placed in the fridge for the first prove. The yeast will still activate and double the size of the dough, but at a much slower rate. It can be kept in the fridge for up to 24 hours. Then simply take it out, knock it back and shape it as normal. You could shape it in the morning, pop it back in the fridge for the second prove and bake it when you get home, giving you a delicious fresh loaf in time for dinner. For more tips on proving dough, see Opposites attract rye rolls (page 84).

The freezer is another great tool for making bread. Yeast quite happily survives the freezing process. Make and shape a loaf, but don't second prove it – pop it in the freezer instead. When you fancy fresh bread for breakfast, take the loaf out of the freezer before you go to bed. It will thaw and prove overnight. Bake it when you get up in the morning.

When is dough proved?
The first clue is that the dough will have doubled in size. If you gently prod it, it should spring back and the indent should vanish pretty quickly. This shows that the gluten strands are holding gas (produced by the yeast) yet are flexible enough to allow the gas to bounce back.

If the dough springs back very quickly, then let it prove a little longer to avoid underproving. Baking an underproved dough will result in a dense crumb.

If the dough doesn't spring back at all, then it is probably overproved. If that has happened, knock it back and reshape it. Trying to bake an overproved dough will result in it deflating in the oven.

CHAPTER 1
Cakes

JAMMY
CENTRE!

1. **Bakewell cherry cupcakes**
   Lemon and almond sponge
   cupcakes with a raspberry jam
   centre. Topped with an amaretto
   liqueur icing and a glacé cherry.

2. **Black cat cupcakes**
   Liquorice and chocolate-
   flavoured cupcakes topped
   with black icing, decorated
   with a cat's face and chocolate
   stand-up ears.

3. **Very berry loaf cake**
   A simple lemon loaf tin cake with
   hidden berries inside. Topped
   with lemon and honey icing,
   a selection of seasonal berries,
   mint leaves and a drizzle
   of honey.

CHARGRILLED
NECTARINES

4. **Lemon & sultana bundt cake**
   A traditional bundt coffee cake
   filled with sultanas and topped
   with lemon icing and crystallized
   lemon rind.

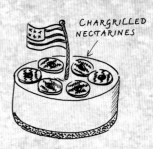

SALT
FLAKE

TEQUILA!

5. **Tequila slammer cheesecakes**
   A very adult after-dinner
   dessert, great for a party. Mini
   lime cheesecakes topped with a
   flake of sea salt, lime jelly and
   a shot of tequila in a pipette.

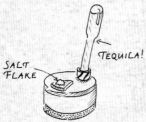

6. Carrot & cardamom cake
A two-layer carrot cake with an orange cream cheese frosting, decorated with candied walnuts and pecans.

7. Rose & pistachio Battenberg cake
Persian-inspired traditional Battenberg with a strawberry jam filling and white marzipan outer.

8. New York cheesecake with chargrilled nectarines
A classic creamy, white, baked cheesecake with a cinnamon-flavoured biscuit base and sultanas. Topped with griddled nectarines.

9. Fruity almond cake
A round cake made from an almond-flavoured sponge topped with plums, apricots and figs.

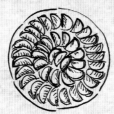

GREAT FOR NEW YEAR'S EVE

FONDANT ROSE AND LEAVES

10. Upside-down toffee apple cake
An upside-down cake with caramelized toffee apple slices.

11. New Year chocolate & raspberry angel food cake
Light and airy chocolate angel cake covered in a chocolate ganache and decorated with white chocolate swirls and gold-leafed raspberries.

12. Chocolate & amaretto prinsesstårta
A twist on the stunning traditional Swedish domed cake.

13. Orange & aniseed layer cake
A show-stopping three-layered cake with honey whipped cream and orange marmalade fillings. Topped with crystallized orange peel.

14. Two-day Christmas fruit cake
A perfectly moist Christmas cake baked, fed and decorated in just 2 days, without the need for weeks of preparation or feeding.

Bakewell cherry cupcakes

These little cakes pay homage to the Cherry Bakewell, a tart that is thought to originate in Bakewell in Derbyshire in the mid-1800s. The Cherry Bakewell had an almond-flavoured fondant topping with a single half glacé cherry on top. These cupcakes are made from lemon- and almond-flavoured sponge with a raspberry jam centre, topped with an amaretto-flavoured icing. If you want to make them for children, replace the liqueur with an extra teaspoon of almond extract and lemon juice. If you are low on time, it's fine to use good-quality shop-bought raspberry jam.

Take a little time when icing them to fill them all consistently and gently press a whole glacé cherry bang in the centre. I always take a box of these when going to visit friends or need to make an entrance. They never fail to impress on all levels!

MAKES 12

Time required: 30 minutes preparation and 30 minutes to ice and decorate

Baking time:
20–25 minutes, plus cooling

Optimum oven position and setting: below centre and fan

Essential equipment:
A 12-hole muffin tin
12 greaseproof paper muffin cases. The ones I use have a bottom diameter of 50mm, top diameter of 80mm and are 44mm high. I use white cases, as I like the stark look of the cherries on an all-white backdrop.
A cupcake corer will cut out a neat well for the jam, but if you don't have one, carefully use a small, sharp knife instead.

INGREDIENTS
150g soft unsalted butter
150g caster sugar
100g self-raising flour
120g ground almonds
3 medium eggs
1 tsp baking powder
finely grated zest of
    1 unwaxed lemon
1 tsp almond extract
1 tbsp milk

For the filling
raspberry jam (page 26)
    made with 100g fresh
    raspberries and
    1 tbsp lemon juice, or use
    150g shop-bought jam

For the icing
400g icing sugar
1 tsp almond extract
2 tbsp amaretto liqueur
juice of 1 lemon, strained
    (use the lemon that
    was zested earlier)
12 glacé cherries – use
    different colours for
    the wow factor

METHOD
Preheat the oven to 160°C fan/180°C/320°F/gas 4. Place a muffin case in each hole of your muffin tin.

Cream together the butter and sugar until pale and fluffy; this takes about 5 minutes in a kitchen mixer fitted with a paddle, or a little longer with a hand mixer. Add the flour, almonds, eggs, baking powder, lemon zest, almond extract and milk, and mix well until combined.

Next, I put the cake mixture into a disposable piping bag, cut the end off the piping bag and pipe the mixture into each muffin case (see tip). Don't fill each case more than halfway – we want the sponge to rise but leave room at the top of the case to hold a good quantity of icing later on. Bake for 20–25 minutes until the tops are firm and a skewer inserted in the centre comes out completely clean.

Remove the cakes from the oven, take them out of the tin and immediately place them on a wire rack to cool.

Once completely cooled, use a cupcake corer to remove a piece of sponge from the centre of each cake. Fill the hole with about 1 teaspoon of jam and push the core back in.

To make the icing, place the icing sugar, almond extract and amaretto in a bowl. Add the lemon juice a little at a time and stir until you have a thick, smooth, glossy icing. Add a few drops of water if you don't have enough lemon juice to achieve the right consistency.

continues overleaf...

Spoon some icing on the top of each cake, until it's perfectly level with the top of the case, and place a whole glacé cherry in the middle of each one. Take your time here and make them all look the same for a stunning set of cupcakes. Leave the icing to set for a couple of hours or overnight before enjoying.

TIPS

Variation
AMARETTO BUTTERCREAM TOPPING
If you prefer your cupcakes with a traditional buttercream topping, try the buttercream recipe on page 23.
Use 250g of unsalted butter and add 2 tablespoons of amaretto liqueur for a great hit of almond flavour.

Putting cake mixture into cupcake cases
Forget spoons and ice cream scoops. For mess-free control, simply put the mixture into a disposable piping bag, snip off the end to make a hole about 2cm wide, and then pipe it into your cases. The piping bag allows perfect control and makes it much easier to put an equal amount of mixture into each case.

About cupcake cases
Have you ever wondered why cupcakes peel away from their paper cases? It's because of moisture. The way to stop it happening is to remove them from the muffin tin as soon as they come out of the oven. If you let them cool in the tin, condensation builds on the outside of the cases, which can cause them to peel away. Also, allow them to cool completely before putting them in an airtight container.

Black cat cupcakes

Here's a fun Halloween bake. Liquorice and chocolate might sound a bit odd, but it really works. The tops are cheekily decorated to look like black cats. Just make sure you don't hand them out to trick or treaters, or you may end up with a queue outside your house.

MAKES 12

Time required: 30 minutes preparation and 45 minutes to ice and decorate

Baking time:
20–25 minutes, plus cooling

Optimum oven position and setting: below centre and fan

Essential equipment:
A 12-hole muffin tin
12 greaseproof paper muffin cases. The ones I use are dark brown and have a bottom diameter of 45mm, top diameter of 80mm and are 40mm high.
A baking sheet; mine is aluminium and measures 38 x 32cm
A disposable piping bag with a 1mm plain round nozzle

INGREDIENTS

150g soft unsalted butter
150g caster sugar
100g self-raising flour
35g plain flour
40g unsweetened cocoa powder
3 medium eggs
2 tsp liquorice extract
1 tbsp milk

For the chocolate ganache
150g dark chocolate, coarsely chopped
250ml double cream
black food colouring gel

METHOD

Preheat the oven to 160°C fan/180°C/320°F/gas 4. Place a muffin case in each hole of your muffin tin. Line the baking sheet with non-stick baking parchment.

First make the chocolate ears decoration. Put the dark chocolate in a heatproof bowl placed over a saucepan of simmering water until melted; make sure the water doesn't touch the bottom of the bowl. Alternatively melt it in a microwave on low for a few minutes. Place it in a piping bag fitted with a 1mm plain round nozzle and let it cool for 5 minutes. Pipe 12 pairs of cat's ears onto the baking parchment; the base of each should be about 2.5cm wide. Place in the fridge to set.

Cream together the butter and sugar until pale and fluffy; this takes about 5 minutes in a kitchen mixer fitted with a paddle, or a little longer with a hand mixer. Add both flours, the cocoa, eggs, liquorice extract and milk, and mix well until combined.

Put the cake mixture into a disposable piping bag, cut the end off the piping bag and pipe the mixture into each muffin case (see tip on page 36). Don't fill each case over halfway. Bake for 20–25 minutes until the tops are firm and a skewer inserted in the centre comes out clean.

Remove the cakes from the oven, take them out of the tin and immediately place on a wire rack to cool. If the cakes have domed above the cases, wait until they are cool, then trim them flat with a small knife.

To make the chocolate ganache, put the chocolate in a heatproof bowl. Bring the cream to the boil in a small saucepan, pour over the chocolate and leave to stand for 10 minutes.

Add a little black food colouring gel and stir the mixture using a spatula until smooth and glossy. Add more food colouring to darken the mixture if necessary.

Put the cakes back into the muffin tin so the cases don't distort when you pour in the ganache. While the ganache is still warm, pour a little onto each cake until level with the top of the case. Pop the tin into the fridge for 30 minutes to firm up the ganache.

Put the white chocolate in a heatproof bowl placed over a saucepan of simmering water until melted. Make sure the water doesn't touch the bottom of the bowl. Alternatively, melt it in a microwave on low for a few minutes. Place it in a disposable piping bag fitted with a 1mm plain round nozzle and let it cool for 30 minutes. Only pipe it when it has firmed up and you have to squeeze it out of the bag rather than it pouring out.

Pipe a cat's face on the ganache using the white chocolate and gently push a pair of ears vertically into the ganache on each cake. Store in the fridge until required.

Very berry loaf cake

This is a really simple yet tasty cake with hidden berries, revealed when you slice through it. The pale sponge is lemon and honey flavoured and the outside of the cake turns dark, giving it a wonderful caramelized flavour. The cake is drizzled with lemon and honey icing and then decorated with blackberries and raspberries with a few mint leaves. A final drizzle of honey over the fruit finishes it off perfectly. Perfect as an afternoon tea treat.

SERVES 6–8

Time required: 30 minutes preparation and 20 minutes to ice and decorate

Baking time:
40–50 minutes, plus cooling

Optimum oven position and setting: centre and fan

Essential equipment:
A 900g/2lb loaf tin (the base of mine measures 95 x 195mm and the tin is 70mm high). Grease and line it with non-stick baking parchment (see tip)

INGREDIENTS

225g soft unsalted butter
185g caster sugar
4 medium eggs
225g self-raising flour
finely grated zest of
    2 unwaxed lemons and
    juice of 1
40g runny honey,
    plus 1 tbsp for icing
150g blackberries
150g raspberries
100g icing sugar
few sprigs of fresh mint

METHOD

Preheat the oven to 160°C fan/180°C/320°F/gas 4.

Cream together the butter and sugar until pale and fluffy; this takes about 5 minutes in a kitchen mixer fitted with a paddle, or a little longer with a hand mixer.

Crack the eggs into a bowl and give them a quick mix. Slowly add them to the butter and sugar mixture, along with 1 tablespoon of the flour, beating all the time.

Next add the lemon zest, the honey and the remaining flour. Give it all a really good mix until well incorporated. Put about half of the cake mixture into the prepared tin and level it out with a spatula.

Place 2 rows of blackberries (about 10 berries) and 1 row of raspberries (about 4 berries) on the mixture. Gently put the rest of the mixture into the tin and place another row of berries on top; gently push them down so they are just visible.

Bake in the centre of the oven for 40–50 minutes, until a skewer inserted in the centre comes out clean. The cake should feel firm to the touch and not wobbling. I place a piece of foil loosely over the cake for the last 10 minutes or so to stop it getting too dark. Don't worry, though, this cake is meant to have a dark caramelized crust.

Leave the cake to cool in the tin for about 10 minutes, then tip it out upside down onto a wire rack to cool completely.

To make the icing, juice one of the zested lemons and strain the juice. Place the icing sugar and 1 tablespoon of honey into a bowl. Add the lemon juice a little at a time until you have a thick, glossy icing. If you add too much liquid and it goes too runny, just add a little more icing sugar.

Place the cake on your presentation plate and drizzle over the icing. I use a disposable piping bag, but you could use a spoon. Take your time and decorate the top of the cake with the rest of the berries and a few mint leaves. Dip a teaspoon into the jar of honey and lightly drizzle over the fruit for an amazing finish.

TIP *Lining a loaf tin*

When making a cake in a loaf tin, I use bulldog clips to hold the lining parchment in place around the top of the tin while I make the cake and take them off just before popping it in the oven.

Lemon & sultana bundt cake

Is there anything prettier than a bundt in the world of coffee cakes? I don't think so! This is a really easy recipe that works every time, no matter how intricate the tin. Most of the bundt tins on the market hold exactly the same volume of batter, so this recipe will work with any standard bundt tin. Take your time to grease the tin really well, then coat the tin with ground almonds, which give the cake a beautiful bronzed finish to complement the icing and crystallized lemon rind. Instead of almonds, you could also use plain flour.

SERVES 12

Time required: 30 minutes prep; 20 minutes to decorate

Baking time: 60 minutes, plus cooling

Optimum oven position and setting: centre and fan

Essential equipment:
A 24cm diameter bundt tin
A strip zester

INGREDIENTS

225g soft unsalted butter
500g caster sugar
4 large eggs
380g plain flour
1 tbsp baking powder
1 tsp fine salt
120ml buttermilk
120ml lemon juice
170g sultanas, tossed in flour
  to stop them sinking
finely grated zest of
  2 unwaxed lemons

To prepare the bundt tin
50g unsalted butter, softened
40g ground almonds

Limoncello icing/decoration
2 unwaxed lemons
100ml water
150g granulated sugar
100g icing sugar
1 tbsp limoncello liqueur
  (or lemon juice)

METHOD

Preheat the oven to 170°C fan/190°C/ 340°F/gas 5.

The first step to success with any bundt is preparation of the tin. Spending time doing this will ensure that the cake will pop out in one perfect piece. Brush the butter all over the inside of the tin. Be generous, and make sure every single bit is coated. Tip in the ground almonds and move the tin around to coat every nook and cranny, then give the tin a good knock out to get rid of excess.

To make the cake, cream together the butter and sugar until pale and fluffy; this takes about 5 minutes in a kitchen mixer fitted with a paddle, or a little longer with a hand mixer.

Slowly add the eggs to the butter and sugar mixture, along with 1 tablespoon of the flour, mixing all the time until incorporated. Then add all the other ingredients and beat them in. Don't overwork the mixture, just make sure it's all well mixed. Pour it evenly into the prepared tin and spread it around with a spatula. Give the tin a couple of sharp knocks on your work surface to get the batter into every part of the tin.

Bake in the centre of the oven for 60 minutes. Do not be tempted to open the oven until at least 45 minutes have gone by. After 45 minutes, place a piece of foil loosely over the tin to stop the top getting too brown.

While the cake is baking, make the toppings. Using a strip zester, take the zest off the lemons so you end up with pieces 3–4cm long. (If you are not using limoncello for the icing, juice the lemons and strain the juice.) Place the zest strips into a pan with the water and 100g of the granulated sugar. Bring to the boil and simmer for 15 minutes. Put the rest of the granulated sugar on a plate. Drain the zest, tip it onto the sugar and stir it all around to coat it. Spread it apart and set aside to dry.

To make the icing, put the icing sugar in a bowl with the limoncello and mix until thick, smooth and glossy. Add a little water or lemon juice if it's too thick, but if it's too thin it will run straight off the cake.

After 60 minutes, check the cake: a skewer inserted into the centre should come out completely clean and the cake should feel firm to the touch. It may need a couple more minutes.

Now here's the key to success. Take the cake out of the oven and leave it to cool in the tin for 10 minutes. If you try and tip it out sooner it could fall apart. When ready, put a wire rack on top of the tin and flip it over. The tin should lift away cleanly.

Let the cake cool completely before dribbling the icing over the cake and placing the candied zest all over top. I always use a (disposable) piping bag to put the icing on a cake as it gives more control.

TIP **Adding dried or glacé fruits to cake mixes**

When adding dried fruits to cake mixtures, always give them a dusting in plain flour first. This will help stop them all sinking to the bottom. Glacé cherries are best washed, dried, quartered and then dusted in flour.

Tequila slammer cheesecakes

Here we have my very adult, very cheeky tequila cheesecakes. I remember the first time I made these for dessert at a dinner party. That night is still fondly talked about now. We had a scream. Have some spare tequila on the side – friends will inevitably want to fill the pipettes again!

MAKES 12 MINI CHEESECAKES

Time required: 75 minutes preparation, plus setting

Essential equipment:
A 12-well non-stick mini-cake tin with loose bottoms
12 food-safe plastic pipettes to hold the tequila
A small kitchen blowtorch

INGREDIENTS

For the base
300g digestive biscuits crushed to fine crumbs
120g unsalted butter, melted

For the cheesecake
6 café curl biscuits
50g dark chocolate, coarsely chopped
3½ sheets gelatine
80ml boiling water
120ml double cream
250g full-fat cream cheese
75g caster sugar
finely grated zest of 2 unwaxed lemons
3 tsp lemon essence

For the topping
4 sheets gelatine
125ml strained lime juice (about 5 limes)
40ml water
25g caster sugar
green food colouring gel
1 lime
1 tbsp coarse sea salt flakes
200ml tequila

NOTE

Take the cream cheese out of the fridge a couple of hours before you want to make the cheesecakes so it reaches room temperature. Try to match the setting strength of the gelatine I use; 4 of the leaves of the gelatine sets 470ml of liquid.

METHOD

To make the base, weigh a mixing bowl, then place the crumbs in the bowl and pour over the melted butter. Stir until well mixed.

Place 25g of the biscuit mix in each of the 12 wells and pack down level and firm. Place the tin in the fridge to set.

Carefully cut the café curl biscuits in half, using a finely serrated knife. Set aside.

Put the chocolate into a heatproof bowl placed over a saucepan of simmering water until melted (make sure the water doesn't touch the bottom of the bowl). Alternatively melt it in a microwave on low for a few minutes.

Take the tin out of the fridge. Dip the end of one of the curl biscuits into the chocolate. Using a brush, paint the bottom 4cm of each curl with melted chocolate. Using the chocolate as glue, stick the curl to the biscuit base and the edge of a well; the tube should be pointing upwards. This tube will hold a pipette of tequila. Repeat for all 12 and set aside.

To make the cheesecake filling, put the gelatine sheets in a bowl of cold water for 5 minutes to soften them. Squeeze the

sheets to remove excess water and place them in a clean bowl. Pour over the boiling water and leave to dissolve.

Put the cream in a mixing bowl and whisk until soft peaks form.

Put the cream cheese and sugar in another mixing bowl and whisk until the sugar has dissolved. Whisk in the lemon zest and essence. Stir the gelatine liquid into the cheese mixture until well combined, then stir in the whipped cream.

Place an equal amount of filling into each well on top of the biscuit base and around the curl. Make sure the top of the filling is level and about 5mm below the top of the wells. Place in the fridge for a couple of hours to set.

To make the topping, put the gelatine sheets in a bowl of cold water for 5 minutes to soften them. Squeeze the sheets to remove excess water and place them in a clean bowl.

Put the lime juice, water and sugar in a small saucepan over a low heat and warm gently – do not boil. Take off the heat. Squeeze the gelatine sheets to remove excess water, put them in the saucepan and stir until they dissolve. Pour the mixture into a clear heatproof jug and add a little green food colouring gel until you achieve a lime colour. Set aside to cool to room temperature.

Slice the lime into 3mm thick slices. Cut a couple of slices into small wedges; you need 12.

When the cheesecakes have set, take them out of the fridge. Place a wedge of lime on top of each one, opposite the curl tube. Very carefully pour a little of the cooled lime juice mixture onto each cheesecake so it reaches just below the top of each well. Place back in the fridge to set – this should take about 2 hours.

When ready to serve, take the cheesecakes out of the fridge. To release them from the tin, use a blowtorch to very quickly and gently warm the outside and bottom of each well. They should be easy to push up and the loose bottoms should also come away.

Place a pinch of sea salt flakes on top of each lime wedge. Fill the 12 pipettes with tequila and put one in each curl tube. Serve immediately.

Carrot & cardamom cake

This is the daddy of all cakes as far as I'm concerned. It is said that the carrot cake dates back to medieval times and was originally known as a carrot pudding. Carrot was used as a sweetener in Britain when sugar was hard to come by. Nowadays sugar is also used, but the carrot gives the cake an amazingly moist texture.

My two-layered version includes raisins and a mixture of different spices in the sponge mix. It is completely shrouded in a cream cheese frosting, and topped with candied walnuts and pecans.

SERVES 10

Time required: 40 minutes prep; 20 minutes to decorate

Baking time:
30–35 minutes, plus cooling

Optimum oven position and setting: below centre and fan

Essential equipment:
Two 23cm/9 inch non-stick springform cake tins, greased and lined with non-stick baking parchment

INGREDIENTS
340g carrots, peeled and finely grated
200g seedless raisins
8 green cardamom pods
3 large eggs
150g caster sugar
50g soft light brown sugar
180ml corn oil
1 tsp vanilla extract
finely grated zest of 2 oranges
180g plain flour
1 tsp baking powder
½ tsp fine salt
1½ tsp ground cinnamon, plus extra for dusting
½ tsp ground ginger

For the frosting
600g full-fat soft cream cheese
300g icing sugar
250ml double cream

For the candied nuts
150g granulated sugar
150ml water
30 walnut halves
30 pecan halves

METHOD
Preheat the oven to 160°C fan/180°C/ 320°F/gas 4.

Squeeze out any excess liquid from the carrots and place them in a bowl. Stir in the raisins and set aside.

Crack open the cardamom pods and crush the seeds to a powder, using a mortar and pestle. Set aside.

Weigh your empty mixing bowl and make a note of it. Put the eggs and both sugars into the bowl and whisk for 4–5 minutes until thick and the whisk leaves a thick ribbon trail when lifted out.

Add the corn oil, vanilla and orange zest, and beat well for a minute.

Sift together the flour, baking powder, salt, cinnamon, ginger and cardamom. Gradually add this to the cake mixture, beating well between each addition until well mixed. Don't overwork the mixture. Fold in the grated carrots and raisins, using a large metal spoon, until evenly mixed.

Weigh your bowl again and subtract the weight of the empty bowl. Divide the mixture evenly between the two prepared tins by placing them on your scales when pouring it in. Place both tins in the oven on the same shelf.

Bake for 30–35 minutes. Check the cakes after 30 minutes: a skewer inserted into the centre should come out completely clean and the cakes should have shrunk away from the sides slightly. They may need a couple more minutes.

continues overleaf...

Leave the cakes to cool in the tins for 10 minutes, then remove and place on a wire rack to cool completely.

To make the candied nuts, place the sugar and water in a saucepan and bring to the boil. Tip in the nuts and simmer for 15 minutes. Line a baking sheet with non-stick baking parchment. Using a slotted spoon, lift the nuts out and place them on the baking sheet to dry.

To make the cream cheese frosting, place the cream cheese in a large mixer bowl and whisk until fluffy. Add the icing sugar and whisk until well mixed and smooth. Pour in the cream and whisk until it becomes thick yet spreadable. Take care not to over-whisk, or it could split.

To assemble the cake, place one of the sponges on your serving plate or cake stand. If it has a slight dome, place it upside down and it should flatten. I don't trim the tops of cakes like this as we can easily hide the dome with the filling and decoration. However, feel free to do so if you want to.

Spread an even layer of the cream cheese frosting, about 1cm/½ inch thick, over the sponge. Place the second sponge gently on top. Using a palette knife, spread the remaining frosting around the sides and top of the cake to cover it completely. (If you put it on a cake turntable, you can make a really cool swirl pattern using the tip of your palette knife and spinning the cake while you move the knife slowly towards the centre.)

Using a fine sieve, give the cake a really light dusting of cinnamon, then place the candied nuts on the top in a concentric design. Keep this cake refrigerated. It will keep for 2 days.

Rose & pistachio Battenberg cake

I've given the traditional Battenberg cake a Persian twist by flavouring the sponges with rose and pistachio. It's a really fragrant combination that complements the strawberry jam and almond marzipan perfectly.

You get a little bite, too, from the pistachios in one of the sponges. I colour the sponges green and pink to match the flavours.

SERVES 8

Time required: 30 minutes prep; 30 minutes to decorate

Baking time:
30–35 minutes, plus cooling

Optimum oven position and setting: below centre and fan

Essential equipment:
I use a Battenberg cake tin, but you can use a 20cm/ 8 inch square cake tin divided in half using baking parchment (see method)

INGREDIENTS

To prepare the tin
20g soft unsalted butter
20g plain flour

For the cake mixture
40g pistachio kernels
175g soft unsalted butter
175g caster sugar
3 medium eggs
175g self-raising flour
green food colouring gel
½ tsp rose water (if you don't like rose flavour, substitute 1 tsp vanilla extract)
pink food colouring gel

To finish
a little icing sugar for dusting
450g white marzipan
5 tbsp smooth strawberry jam

METHOD

Preheat the oven to 160°C fan/170°C/ 320°F/gas 4.

Grease the Battenberg tin really well with butter, then coat it with flour. If using a square cake tin, grease and line it with non-stick baking parchment. Fold a pleat down the centre of the parchment (it should look like an upside-down T shape) and use the parchment to divide the tin into two halves.

Pulse the pistachio kernels in a food processor until very fine. Alternatively place them in a bag and hit them with a rolling pin until finely crushed.

Weigh your empty mixing bowl and make a note of it. In the mixing bowl, cream together the butter and sugar until pale and fluffy; this takes about 5 minutes in a kitchen mixer fitted with a paddle, or a little longer with a hand mixer.

Slowly add the eggs to the creamed butter and sugar, along with 1 tablespoon of the flour, mixing all the time until incorporated. Fold in the remaining flour until well mixed.

Weigh the mixing bowl and subtract the weight of the empty bowl. You can now work out how much mixture you have. Place half of the mixture into another bowl.

Fold the ground pistachios and a hint of green colouring into one half of the mixture

until well blended and evenly coloured. Add the rose water (or vanilla essence) and a hint of the pink colouring to the other half of the mixture and fold in until well blended and evenly coloured. Place the pink mixture in one half of the tin and the pistachio mixture in the other half.

Bake for 30–35 minutes until well risen and a skewer inserted in the centre comes out clean. Remove from the oven and leave to cool completely in the tin.

Lightly dust your work surface with icing sugar and roll out the marzipan to about 3mm thick. You need a piece about 35 x 25cm to cover the cake.

Remove the two sponges from the tin. Cut each sponge in half lengthways. Gently warm the strawberry jam in a small pan or the microwave. Use the warmed jam to stick together the four strips of cake to make a chequerboard effect.

Trim one long side of your marzipan straight, using a ruler and knife. Brush the top and sides of the assembled cake with jam and place upside down on the straight edge of your rolled-out marzipan. Brush the bottom of the cake with jam and now roll the cake over until completely covered in marzipan. Trim away the excess marzipan and trim the ends of the cake using a sharp serrated knife. Place on your presentation plate and enjoy.

New York cheesecake with chargrilled nectarines

I do love a New York cheesecake. A great one – creamy and rich with vanilla – can send you into cheesecake heaven. This is the one I remember from my childhood, loaded with sultanas and a cinnamon-flavoured biscuit base. For that extra flavour dimension and wow factor, it has griddled nectarines on the top.

Make this cheesecake the day before you need it and keep it in the fridge overnight to firm up. Take the cream cheese out of the fridge a couple of hours before you want to make the cheesecake so it reaches room temperature.

SERVES 12

Time required: 45 minutes preparation

Baking time:
60–75 minutes, plus cooling and overnight chilling

Optimum oven position and setting: centre and fan

Essential equipment:
A 23cm/9 inch non-stick springform cake tin. Or a cake tin with a loose bottom and silicone seal. Grease well and line the base with non-stick baking parchment.
A kitchen mixer with paddle attachment
A non-stick ridged griddle pan

INGREDIENTS

For the base
200g digestive biscuits, crushed to fine crumbs
2 tsp ground cinnamon
120g unsalted butter, melted

For the cheesecake
840g full-fat soft cream cheese
300g caster sugar
40g cornflour
1 tsp vanilla paste
finely grated zest of 2 unwaxed lemons
3 large eggs, beaten
230ml double cream
100g sultanas (optional), tossed in flour to stop them sinking

For the chargrilled nectarines
4 semi-ripe nectarines

METHOD

Preheat the oven to 170°C fan/190°C/ 340°F/gas 5.

To make the base, place the crushed biscuits in a bowl, add the cinnamon and pour over the melted butter. Stir until well mixed. Press the mixture into the base of the tin in an even layer. Bake for 10 minutes, then place on a wire rack while you make the cheesecake filling.

In your mixer bowl place 280g of the cream cheese, 100g of the sugar and the cornflour. Mix for about 4 minutes until well creamed. Add the rest of the cream cheese in three batches, mixing well between each one. Add the rest of the sugar, the vanilla and lemon zest, and mix for a minute. Slowly add the eggs, while mixing continuously. Pour in the cream and tip in the sultanas. Using a large metal spoon, gently fold in until incorporated.

If you are using a springform tin, place it on a large piece of kitchen foil and bring the foil up around the sides to stop water from the water bath leaking into the cheesecake. (I use a cake tin with a loose bottom that has a silicone seal.)

Pour the cheesecake mixture over the cooled biscuit base and place in a roasting tin. Put this in the lower half of the oven and pour boiling water into the tin so it comes about 2.5cm up the side of the tin.

Bake for 60–75 minutes. After 30 minutes, gently rest a piece of greased foil over the cheesecake to stop the top browning too much. The cheesecake is ready when the centre is still just wobbling. The most accurate way of checking is by using a temperature probe: the centre of the cheesecake should be just over 70°C/160°F. It will set firm as it cools.

When ready, turn the oven off and open the oven door. Leave the cheesecake in the oven for 20 minutes to cool gradually. This will help prevent cracking in the top of the cheesecake.

Take the cheesecake out of the oven and out of the water bath. Place it on a wire rack for a couple of hours to cool completely. Place in the fridge overnight.

To make the chargrilled nectarines, place a griddle pan over a high heat. Cut each nectarine in half and remove the stone. Cut into 5mm/¼ inch segments. Place the segments in the hot pan and turn over after about a minute. Set aside to cool for 10 minutes before placing them on the cheesecake.

When ready to serve, pop the cheesecake from the tin but leave it on the tin base and place it on your serving plate. Place the cooled nectarines on the top.

Fruity almond cake

This cake is incredibly easy to make, yet looks amazing. It has a wonderful almond-flavoured crust but is really moist, golden and buttery inside. The fruits on top caramelize during the bake, retaining some of their bite. It's a great cake to give as a gift or just enjoy a slice with a cup of tea.

SERVES 8

Time required: 40 minutes preparation

Baking time: 50–60 minutes, plus cooling

Optimum oven position and setting: centre and fan

Essential equipment: A 23cm/9 inch non-stick springform cake tin, greased and lined with non-stick baking parchment

INGREDIENTS

200g soft unsalted butter
150g caster sugar
50g soft brown sugar
3 medium eggs
180g plain flour
120g ground almonds
2 tsp almond extract
1 tsp baking powder
finely grated zest of 1 orange
finely grated zest of
    1 unwaxed lemon
1 tbsp milk
3 tbsp thin-cut marmalade

For the topping

1 fresh fig, cut in half
2 fresh apricots, stoned and
    cut in halves
1 plum, stoned and cut in half
20g flaked almonds
2 tbsp icing sugar

METHOD

Preheat the oven to 160°C fan/180°C/ 320°F/gas 4.

Cream together the butter and both sugars until pale and fluffy; this takes about 5 minutes in a kitchen mixer fitted with a paddle, or a little longer with a hand mixer.

Slowly add the eggs to the creamed butter sugar, along with 1 tablespoon of the flour, mixing all the time until incorporated. Add the remaining flour, the almonds, almond extract, baking powder, orange and lemon zest and milk and give it all a really good mix until well incorporated.

Place about half of the mixture into the prepared tin and gently even it out using a spatula. Dot the marmalade evenly on top of the cake mixture. Add the remaining cake mixture to the tin and gently level it with a spatula.

Push the topping fruits lightly into the cake mix (about 1cm in is enough) in a concentric design. They will naturally sink slightly and the cake will rise around them. Scatter the flaked almonds between the fruits and, using a fine sieve, dust the icing sugar evenly over the top of everything.

Bake for 50–60 minutes. After 50 minutes, check the cake: a skewer inserted into the centre should come out completely clean and the cake should have shrunk away slightly from the sides of the tin. Beware though, this cake can trick you into thinking it's ready. Touch the centre gently and if it is wobbling it's not ready; it should feel firm. It may need a few more minutes. If it starts to brown too much, gently place a piece of foil over the tin while the cake bakes. Alternatively, use a temperature probe to test when it is baked to perfection: the centre of the cake should be 98°C/208°F.

Leave to cool in the tin for 10 minutes, then remove and place on a wire rack to cool completely.

Upside-down toffee apple cake

I'm a child of the 1970s, when upside-down cakes were all the rage. My take on the classic pineapple upside-down cake is included in the honey chapter (page 206), but why not give this toffee apple version a go too? Let it cool in the tin as this allows the apples to set in place before turning out.

METHOD

Preheat the oven to 160°C fan/180°C/320°F/gas 4.

Setting the apples aside, place all the remaining topping ingredients in a small saucepan and heat gently until well mixed and melted. Do not bring to the boil. Pour into the base of the prepared cake tin and spread it out evenly.

Place the apple wedges on top of this mixture in a single-layer concentric design. Take your time, as it's the showstopping top of the cake, and try not to overlap the apples. Set aside to cool.

To make the cake mixture, cream together the butter and sugar until pale and fluffy; this takes about 5 minutes in a kitchen mixer fitted with a paddle, or a little longer with a hand mixer.

Slowly add the eggs to the butter and sugar mixture, along with 1 tablespoon of the flour, mixing all the time until incorporated. Add the remaining flour, baking powder, milk, Calvados and vanilla, and beat them in. Don't overwork the mixture, just make sure it's all well mixed. Spoon the mixture gently and evenly into the tin and spread it around carefully with a spatula, trying not to disturb the sliced apples (see tip).

Bake in the lower half of the oven for 40–50 minutes. After 40 minutes, check the cake: a skewer inserted into the centre should come out completely clean and the cake should have shrunk away from the sides slightly. It may need a few more minutes.

Let the cake cool in the tin for about 20 minutes, then tip it out upside down onto your serving plate. If the cake is slightly domed, trim it flat with a serrated knife before turning it out.

TIP *Piping cake mixture into a tin*

This recipe requires you to put the sponge mix on top of some neatly arranged apples. We don't want to ruin the design, so here's a quick and easy way to avoid that. Place the cake mixture in a disposable piping bag and snip the end open to about 1.5cm. Pipe the mixture in a spiral, starting from the outside of the tin and ending up in the middle. Gently level the top with a spatula.

SERVES 10

Time required: 40 minutes preparation

Baking time: 40–50 minutes, plus cooling

Optimum oven position and setting: below centre and fan

Essential equipment: A 23cm/9 inch non-stick springform cake tin, greased and lined with non-stick baking parchment

INGREDIENTS

For the toffee apple topping
3 Braeburn apples, peeled, cored and cut into 3mm segments
70g unsalted butter
1½ tsp plain flour
100g soft brown sugar
3 tbsp Calvados or brandy
¼ tsp ground cinnamon
¼ tsp ground cloves

For the cake mixture
225g soft unsalted butter
225g caster sugar
4 medium eggs
225g self-raising flour
½ tsp baking powder
2 tbsp whole milk
2 tbsp Calvados or brandy
1 tsp vanilla extract

New Year chocolate & raspberry angel food cake

This American cake originated in the nineteenth century and gets its name from the light, airy texture that is said to be like the food of angels. My version has cocoa powder added to it, tempering the traditional sweetness of the cake. Coated in a smooth dark chocolate ganache and topped with raspberries adorned with gold leaf, is there a better cake to welcome in the New Year?

It's really simple to make, but you will need an angel food cake tin. This tin has a loose bottom and little feet, as the cake is cooled upside down to help it stay light and fluffy. Don't be tempted to grease the tin; the cake clings to the sides, which helps prevent it deflating.

This cake uses a lot of egg whites, so when making it I buy egg whites in a carton.

SERVES 12

Time required: 60 minutes preparation

Baking time: 40 minutes, plus cooling

Optimum oven position and setting: centre and fan

Essential equipment:
A 25cm/10 inch angel food cake tin
A kitchen mixer fitted with a whisk
A disposable piping bag fitted with a 2mm plain round nozzle

INGREDIENTS
30g unsweetened cocoa powder
50ml boiling water
2 tsp vanilla paste
125g plain flour
350g caster sugar
14 medium egg whites (420g)
2 tsp cream of tartar

For the chocolate ganache
250g dark chocolate, coarsely chopped
250ml double cream

Decoration
50g white chocolate, coarsely chopped
140g fresh raspberries
3 sheets edible gold leaf

METHOD
Preheat the oven to 170°C fan/190°C/340°F/gas 5.

Whisk together the cocoa powder and boiling water in a bowl until smooth. Whisk in the vanilla paste.

Sift together the flour and 140g of the sugar and set aside.

In a spotlessly clean mixing bowl, whisk the egg whites until soft peaks form. Add the cream of tartar and whisk again briefly. Add the remaining caster sugar while whisking until the whites are thick and glossy and form very stiff peaks.

Take a cupful of the egg whites and add to the bowl with the cocoa mixture; whisk together and set aside.

Sift the flour mixture into the egg whites in four batches, using a balloon whisk to gently fold it in. Add the cocoa mixture and gently whisk until well combined. Pour the mixture evenly into the tin and run a knife around the edge to get rid of any air pockets.

Bake for 40 minutes or until a skewer inserted in the centre comes out completely clean. The top of the cake should feel firm and the surface will have cracks like a soufflé. Take the cake out of the oven and immediately turn the tin upside down and leave to cool completely for about 90 minutes.

Remove the cooled cake from the tin. Run a thin palette knife around the outer side of the tin and use a thin, flat skewer to loosen the cake around the centre core. Push the cake out of the tin. Run the palette knife around the base; the cake should come free. Place it on a wire rack with a roasting tin underneath it.

continues overleaf...

To make the chocolate ganache, put the chocolate in a heatproof bowl. Bring the cream to the boil in a small saucepan, pour over the chocolate and leave to stand for 10 minutes.

Using a balloon whisk, stir the mixture until smooth and glossy. While the ganache is still warm pour it over the cake, starting on the top so it runs down the sides and covers it completely. You can use a palette knife to spread the ganache. Set aside to cool.

For the decoration, melt the white chocolate in a small bowl placed over boiling water or in a microwave. Place in a piping bag fitted with a 2mm plain round nozzle and leave to cool and thicken slightly.

Place the cake on your presentation plate. Pipe a design on the top of the cake using the white chocolate and then place a ring of raspberries around the outer edge. Place a little gold leaf on each raspberry, using a small brush.

TIP *Recovering a split chocolate ganache*

Sometimes when making a chocolate ganache it will split, due to the fat from the cream separating. I also find that the higher the cocoa content in the chocolate the more susceptible it is to splitting. To recover a split ganache, whisk in a little boiling water, 1 tablespoon at a time, and the mixture will emulsify and become smooth again. Don't be tempted to add cream or milk, as that will make it worse.

Chocolate & amaretto prinsesstårta

I was brought up on Hillgate in Stockport in the 1970s. Every Saturday morning my mum used to go shopping into the centre of Stockport. I remember dreading it sometimes as we didn't have a car, so it involved a rather long walk down to the town centre, come rain or shine. However, the route always took us past a bakery on St Petersgate called The Golden Door. It literally did have a golden-mirrored door and the window was always full of delicious-looking cakes and breads. Mum would always treat me to a chocolate truffle covered in chocolate sprinkles. But the most amazing thing I remember was the bright green domed cream cake with a pink rose on top that sat proudly in the window. Every now and then, mum would buy one to take home for us all to enjoy. This cake stayed in my memory.

Then, many years later, the Bake Off came along and I found myself in a technical challenge, being asked to make a Swedish prinsesstårta. I had no idea what that was until I started reading the instructions, and sure enough it was the green domed cake I remembered from my childhood. The granddaughter of the baker at The Golden Door got in touch with me recently and told me the entire family used to call it the Kermit cake!

My twist on this classic has a chocolate-flavoured sponge and a chocolate crème pâtissière filling, generously topped with an amaretto-flavoured whipped cream. You can make the crème pâtissière and the jam in advance. This cake has quite a few processes, but trust me, it's a real showstopper and tastes delicious.

SERVES 12

Time required: about 2 hours preparation, plus 45 minutes freezing

Baking time:
25–30 minutes, plus cooling

Optimum oven position and setting: below centre and fan

Essential equipment:
A 23cm/9 inch non-stick springform cake tin, greased and lined with non-stick baking parchment
Disposable piping bags fitted with a small plain round nozzle and a small star nozzle

INGREDIENTS

75g plain flour
75g cornflour
20g unsweetened cocoa powder
1 tsp baking powder
4 large eggs
140g caster sugar
50g unsalted butter, melted
1 tsp almond extract

For the filling
1 quantity (approx. 900g) of chocolate crème pâtissière (page 22)
800ml double cream
4 tbsp icing sugar
120ml amaretto liqueur

raspberry jam (page 26) made with 100g fresh raspberries and 1 tbsp lemon juice, or use 100g shop-bought jam

For the cake covering
800g white marzipan
green food colouring gel
50g icing sugar for dusting

METHOD

Make the chocolate crème pâtissière and allow to cool completely. You can make this the day before and keep it in the fridge until required.

Preheat the oven to 170°C fan/190°C/ 340°F/gas 5.

To make the sponge, sift together the flour, cornflour, cocoa and baking powder into a bowl.

This next stage is the key to success. Put the eggs and caster sugar into a large bowl and, using an electric mixer, whisk together for about 8 minutes until the mixture is very thick and well risen. The whisk should leave a thick trail when lifted out of the mixture. Doing this will give you a really light and well-risen sponge, thick enough to cut into three layers.

Sift the dry ingredients over the egg mixture in three batches, carefully folding in using a large metal spoon. Do this gently to avoid deflating the mix, but make sure it is well incorporated.

Next, fold in the melted butter and almond essence until just mixed. Pour the mixture gently into the prepared tin and bake for 25–30 minutes until well risen and firm. Test with a skewer inserted into the centre: it should come out clean and the sponge should be firm to the touch. It should also have started to shrink away from the side of the tin.

Remove from the oven and leave to cool completely in the tin before transferring it to a wire rack.

For the filling, put the cream into a large bowl with the icing sugar and whisk until soft peaks form. Add the amaretto liqueur and whisk until just stiff. Set aside.

To assemble, cut the cake horizontally into three even layers, using a sharp serrated knife. Place one of the layers onto your serving plate or cake stand. Spread a very thin layer of the chocolate crème pâtissière over the first sponge.

Place a quarter of the remaining crème pâtissière into a piping bag fitted with a small plain round nozzle and use about half of it to pipe a border around the edge of the sponge. This ring will hold the jam in place. Spoon the jam onto the sponge and spread evenly within the border.

Take a quarter of the whipped cream and fold it into the remaining crème pâtissière. Spread some of it over the jam until you fill the ring completely.

Place the second sponge carefully and gently on top. Pipe another ring of crème pâtissière around the edge and fill with the remaining cream and crème pâtissière mixture.

Place the third sponge carefully and gently on top.

Put about 100ml/3½fl oz of the remaining whipped cream in a piping bag fitted with a small star nozzle and place in the fridge for later.

Using a large palette knife, spread the remaining whipped cream in a thin layer all over the sides of the cake, smoothing into a dome shape on the top of the cake. Place the entire cake in the freezer for about 45 minutes to set the cream dome.

Take the marzipan and add a very small amount of the green colouring. Knead until an even pastel colour is achieved; add a little more colour if required.

Lightly dust a work surface with the icing sugar and roll out the marzipan to a 40cm diameter circle, large enough to cover the cake. Lift the marzipan up over the cake and use your hands to shape the marzipan around the sides of the cake to get a smooth finish. Trim off the excess and reserve the trimmings.

Take the piping bag filled with cream out of the fridge and pipe around the base of the cake.

To finish off, I take the marzipan trimmings and add a little more green colouring to make them darker, then use a leaf cutter to make leaves to decorate the cake. A little edible glue is great for sticking them onto the dome. Depending on the time of year, you could theme the cake and decorate it with snowflakes, bats or flowers, or perhaps a piped design of melted dark chocolate.

Orange & aniseed layer cake

Having been brought up in a Spanish family, the flavour of aniseed played a huge part in the foods I ate. Massively underrated, it is seldom used for cooking in the UK. I remember spice packages being sent over from grandparents in Spain to my parents' home in Stockport. My grandmother had clearly spent many hours packing them and they were enclosed with stitched sackcloth to deter prying eyes. Their arrival was always greeted with excitement. They were full of sweet smoked paprika, aniseeds, saffron, baking powder and El Aeroplano paella seasoning. The Christmas packages would also be packed with delights such as *polvorones* – a kind of Spanish shortbread (see page 228) – and ornate marzipan fruits.

Order yourself some aniseeds and give this recipe a go. For this recipe, I grind them to a powder in a coffee grinder. I tend to do a big batch and then keep the powder in an airtight container.

This high-stacked cake is sure to put a smile on faces as well as introduce some new flavour combinations. Make it a few hours before you need it and it will quite happily live in the fridge. You can even make the sponges the day before you need them and wrap them tightly in clingfilm.

SERVES 12–14

Time required: 60 minutes preparation and 20 minutes to assemble and decorate

Baking time:
30–35 minutes, plus cooling

Optimum oven position and setting: centre, below centre and fan

Essential equipment:
Three 23cm/9 inch non-stick springform cake tins, greased and lined with non-stick baking parchment
Disposable piping bags fitted with a 1cm plain round nozzle and a large star nozzle

INGREDIENTS
280g soft unsalted butter
500g caster sugar
5 large eggs, separated
600g plain flour
5 tsp baking powder
½ tsp fine salt
320ml whole milk
4 tbsp runny honey
25g ground aniseeds
finely grated zest of 8 oranges

For the filling
1 litre double cream
80g runny honey, plus extra for drizzling
200g orange marmalade

Crystallized orange zest decoration
2 oranges
100ml water
150g granulated sugar

METHOD
Preheat the oven to 160°C fan/180°C/320°F/gas 4.

Cream together the butter and 375g of the caster sugar until pale and fluffy; this takes 5 minutes in a kitchen mixer fitted with a paddle, or a little longer with a hand mixer.

Slowly add the egg yolks to the butter and sugar mixture, along with 1 tablespoon of the flour, mixing all the time until incorporated. Add the remaining flour, baking powder, salt, milk, honey, aniseeds and orange zest, and mix until well incorporated.

In a spotlessly clean bowl, whisk the egg whites until soft peaks form, then gradually add the remaining caster sugar until thick and glossy. Using a large metal spoon, gradually fold the egg whites into the cake mixture. Do this gently so as not to lose too much of the air.

Divide the mixture equally among the three prepared tins and place them in the oven. You may have to put two on the centre shelf and the third below them on the bottom shelf.

Bake for 30–35 minutes. After 30 minutes, check the cakes: a skewer inserted into the centre should come out completely clean and the cakes should have shrunk away from the sides slightly. They may need a few more minutes (especially the one on the lower shelf).

continues overleaf…

Leave the cakes to cool in the tins for 10 minutes, then remove and place on a wire rack to cool.

While the cakes are baking, make the filling and decoration.

Using a strip zester, take the zest off the oranges so you end up with pieces 3–4cm long. Place the zest strips into a pan with the water and 100g of the sugar. Bring to the boil and simmer for 15 minutes. Put the rest of the sugar on a plate. Drain the zest, tip it onto the sugar and stir it all around to coat it. Spread it apart and set aside to dry.

To make the filling, put the cream in a large bowl with the honey and whisk just until stiff peaks form. Place two-thirds of the whipped cream in a piping bag fitted with a 1cm plain round nozzle and the remainder in a piping bag fitted with a star nozzle.

Next, assemble the cake. Place one of the sponges onto your serving plate the right way up. There's no need to trim the tops of cakes like this as we can easily hide the dome with the filling and decoration. However, feel free to do so if you want to.

Using a teaspoon, drizzle some honey over the sponge. Spread a thin layer of marmalade over the sponge, using a palette knife. Don't go right to the edge; leave about 2cm uncovered. Using the piping bag with the plain nozzle, pipe rounds of cream all around the edge of the sponge, then fill in the middle.

Place the second sponge gently, top down, on the first layer. Drizzle a little honey, spread a thin layer of marmalade, and pipe cream on this layer exactly as you did for the first sponge.

Take the third sponge and gently place it, top up, on the bottom two layers. Using the piping bag with the star nozzle, pipe cream around the edge of the top layer. Cover the exposed sponge on the top of the cake with a good layer of marmalade. Finish off by placing the crystallized orange zest on the piped cream around the top.

TIP

How to pipe

Piping is daunting for many people setting out on a baking journey. Yes, it's true that practice makes perfect, but there are a couple of things you can do to make it easier. Firstly, make sure that whatever it is you are piping is not runny – otherwise the piping bag will empty itself as soon as you pick it up. The filling should come out when you apply even pressure.

When piping, hold the tip of the nozzle about 1cm above whatever it is you are piping onto. The contents need room to come out and form a shape. After you have piped your shape, stop the pressure and quickly lift the piping bag away to make a neat finish.

Two-day Christmas fruit cake

If ever there was an iconic bake, it's the Christmas cake. Having been around for nearly 150 years, the moist and boozy fondant-covered fruit cake has pleased many generations. Hopefully it will please many more.

I don't want to be a slave to the Christmas cake, though. Weeks of preparation and 'feeding' it with booze just aren't for me. I've tried, but inevitably end up forgetting about it and missing the strict feeding routine. I also find them a little too soggy sometimes, a result of almost overfeeding. I want the cake to be moist, but it must still have a bite and good texture.

So here is my two-day Christmas fruit cake. You can make the cake one evening and decorate it the next. When hardcore cake aficionados ask how long I have fed it for, they are always shocked when I tell them it was made in a total of 2 days. Evening 1, bake the cake, feed and let it cool completely. Seal it up overnight in an airtight container and feed it again the next morning. Decorate it that evening and job done. It will keep as long as a traditionally made and fed fruit cake.

A fruit cake isn't just for Christmas. This recipe is fantastic for birthdays, weddings, celebrations...any time you need a great fruit cake, this fits the bill perfectly.

SERVES 15–20

Time required: 2 hours

Baking time: 2 hours, plus cooling

Optimum oven position and setting: centre and fan

Essential equipment:
A 23cm/9 inch non-stick springform cake tin, greased and lined with non-stick baking parchment
A 30cm diameter cake board

Optional, for decorating:
A fondant icing smoother gives a professional finish
A selection of fondant shape cutters, such as snowflakes
A small pot of edible glue
1 metre of ribbon

INGREDIENTS
For the cake mixture
200g plain flour
1 tsp baking powder
1 tsp mixed spice
1 tsp ground cinnamon
175g unsalted butter
200g soft dark brown sugar
100ml brandy
75ml dark or spiced rum
4 tbsp runny honey
300g sultanas
175g currants
175g raisins
140g dried prunes, cut into quarters
85g glacé cherries, halved
finely grated zest of 1 orange
finely grated zest of 1 unwaxed lemon
3 large eggs, beaten
50g ground almonds

For feeding
8 tbsp cherry brandy

For the topping and decoration
4 tbsp smooth apricot jam
800g ready-to-roll golden marzipan
50g icing sugar for dusting
50g Trex shortening for greasing
800g ready-to-roll white fondant icing
your choice of food colouring gels

METHOD

Preheat the oven to 130°C fan/150°C/ 270°F/gas 2.

Sift together the flour, baking powder and spices in a bowl and set aside.

Put the butter, sugar, brandy, rum and honey in a large pan over a medium heat and stir until the sugar has dissolved. Add the fruits and zests and stir well. Simmer for 10 minutes. Remove from the heat and leave to cool for 40 minutes.

When the mixture has cooled, stir in the eggs and almonds and mix well. Fold in the flour mixture until really well mixed. Pour the mixture into the prepared tin and level it out with a spatula.

Bake for 60 minutes, then turn the oven temperature down to 120°C fan/140°C/250°F/gas 1. Bake for another 60–75 minutes, covering with a piece of foil for the last 30 minutes or so. After a total of 2 hours, check the cake: a skewer inserted into the centre should come out completely clean and the cake should feel firm to the touch. It may need longer.

When it is ready, remove from the cake from the oven and leave to cool in the tin for 15 minutes.

While still in the tin and warm, prick the top of the cake all over with a toothpick. Place 4 tablespoons of cherry brandy in a small bowl and using a pastry brush evenly coat the top of the cake. Leave it to soak in before releasing the cake from the tin and placing on a wire rack to cool completely.

Wrap the cake loosely in baking parchment, then place in an airtight container overnight.

The next morning, brush 4 tablespoons of cherry brandy over the top of the cake and close the container again.

That evening, place the cake on the cake board. Warm the apricot jam in a microwave or small pan and brush all over the cake.

Knead the marzipan gently to soften it a little. Lightly dust your work surface with the icing sugar and roll out the marzipan to a circle about 4mm thick, larger than 40cm diameter, large enough to cover the cake. Lift the marzipan up over the cake and use your hand to shape it around the sides of the cake to get a smooth finish. Trim off the excess.

Clean your work surface and rub a large area with a layer of Trex. Knead the fondant icing gently to soften it a little. Roll out the fondant on the greased surface to a circle about 5mm thick, larger than 40cm diameter, large enough to cover the cake. Brush the marzipan sparingly with a little water, then lift the fondant up over the cake and use your hands to shape it around the sides of the cake to get a smooth finish. Trim off the excess. You can use a fondant icing smoother to get a really professional finish.

Use the trimmings to decorate the cake. You can colour the fondant and use festive fondant shape cutters to make decorations. Dust the surface with icing sugar and roll the fondant to about 2mm thick; dust the cutters with icing sugar to get some really sharp shapes. Stick the decorations to the cake using a small brush and a little edible glue. Finally, wrap a ribbon around the base of the cake and use a couple of pins to secure it.

TIP

Rolling out marzipan and fondant icing

If you're going to do a lot of cake decorating, a long rolling pin is one of the best investments you could make. I have a catering-grade white plastic one that is 50cm long, which makes rolling out so much easier.

To roll out marzipan, I put a good dusting of icing sugar on the surface and then begin to roll. Keep lifting, rotating and flipping it over to stop it sticking and use more icing sugar as necessary. I usually roll it out to a thickness of about 4mm.

When rolling out fondant icing, give your work surface a coating of shortening fat such as Trex. This is flavourless and odourless and will prevent the icing from sticking. It's much better than using icing sugar as it doesn't dry the icing out.

CHAPTER 2
Breads

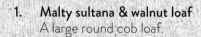

1. **Malty sultana & walnut loaf**
   A large round cob loaf.

GREAT WITH PAELLA

2. **Spelt batons**
   Short batons made with ancient grains.

TEAR AND SHARE!

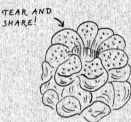

TRY THE SOUP TOO!

3. **Spicy bread bowls & my spicy carrot, parsnip and coriander soup**
   How to make four large paprika and garlic bread bowls. Perfect for soup, stew or a chilli con carne. Alternative to make smaller ones also, for a starter. Recipe for soup included.

4. **Cheshire cheese & onion rolls**
   Traditional small rolls with cheese from my region.

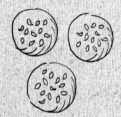

5. Tikka masala breadsticks
Indian spiced fruity
breadsticks.

**6. Garlic & Parmesan
monkey bread**
A monkey bread-style sharing
loaf baked in a bundt tin.

**7. Northern milk loaf with a
Japanese Hokkaido twist**
A traditional Northern
milk loaf shaped with a
Japanese twist.

8. Spiral seed & honey loaf
A traditional white loaf which,
when sliced, reveals a multi-
seed sweet spiral.

SCARY
HALLOWEEN
BREAD

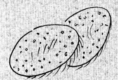

EXPERIMENT
WITH YOUR
OWN TOPPINGS

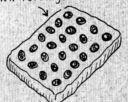

9. Halloween pumpkin seed bread
A round pumpkin seed, sultana
and orange flavoured cob slashed
to look like a carved pumpkin
when it comes out of the oven.

10. Persian pitta breads
Quick and easy spicy pittas,
to eat straight from the oven.

11. Opposites attract rye rolls
Two different spiced rye doughs
(one dark and one light) layered
and rolled to look and taste
spectacular.

12. Ale focaccia
Two yeasty focaccias with
different toppings: the first
olive, and the second onion,
oregano and chilli.

Malty sultana & walnut loaf

This is not as sweet or sticky as a traditional malt loaf. A slice of this is great with either a sweet or savoury topping. Try it as the basis for cheese on toast; you'll never look back. It looks great, too. You will be amazed how easy it is to make bread that looks like it's just come out of an artisan bakery. There's no special equipment needed for shaping, just your hands.

MAKES 1 LOAF

Time required: 30 minutes preparation and two proves

Baking time: 30–35 minutes

Optimum oven position and setting: centre and no fan, with a baking stone

Essential equipment:

A baking sheet; mine is aluminium and measures 38 x 32cm. Line with non-stick baking parchment

A large bag to put the baking sheet into for proving

Optional: proving basket (see tip). To use a proving basket for this recipe, follow the shaping instructions then pop the ball of dough in the prepared basket.

INGREDIENTS

400g strong white bread flour, plus extra for dusting
100g strong wholemeal flour
10g instant yeast
1 tbsp malt extract
1 tbsp soft brown sugar
1 tsp fine salt
320ml cool water
a little rapeseed oil for greasing the proving bowl
120g walnut pieces
120g sultanas

METHOD

Place the flours, yeast, malt extract, sugar and salt in a large bowl. When adding the yeast and salt, put them at opposite sides of the bowl.

Add two-thirds of the water and begin to mix it all together with your fingers – or use a kitchen mixer with a dough hook. Add more water gradually until all the dry ingredients are picked up and you have a soft dough. You may not need all the water.

Tip the mixture out onto a clean surface and knead it for about 8 minutes. You will work through the initial wet stage and eventually end up with a smooth, soft, silky dough. If you are using a kitchen mixer, knead it for about 6 minutes.

Lightly oil a large bowl and place the dough in it. Cover it with clingfilm or a shower cap and leave it on one side until doubled in size. Depending on room temperature, this can take 1 hour, but it'll be fine for 2–3 hours.

When the dough has proved, tip it out onto a lightly floured surface. Using your hands, flatten it out to a large circle and place the sultanas and walnut pieces on it. Fold the dough repeatedly in on itself to evenly distribute the fruit and nuts. You can give it a few gentle kneads to achieve this.

Form the dough into a smooth round cob by repeatedly turning it while constantly tucking it under itself, using your hands. This will give you a tight, smooth top. Place it on the lined baking sheet. Place the baking sheet in a large bag, making sure it

doesn't touch the dough, and leave to prove until doubled in size. This can take a couple of hours, as the yeast has to work hard to push the fruit and nuts up.

While the loaf proves, preheat the oven to 200°C fan/220°C/390°F/gas 7.

When the loaf has risen, dust the top with a little flour, using a fine sieve. Next, use a very sharp knife to carefully make two parallel slashes about 2–3mm deep in the top of the loaf to control how it will grow during baking. Be gentle when making the cuts so as not to deflate the loaf.

Bake for 30–35 minutes. The loaf should be a deep golden colour and sound hollow when tapped. You can test if it is baked to perfection by using a temperature probe: the centre of the loaf should be just over 90°C/195°F. Place on a wire rack to cool.

TIP *Proving baskets*

Proving baskets are widely available and can produce fantastic results. Most come with a cloth liner, but I don't bother with that. Before putting your dough into the basket, give it a really generous dusting with either rye flour or rice flour (or both); these flours will stop your loaf sticking to the basket. After your loaf has risen, don't tip it out onto your baking sheet as the impact could deflate it and undo all your hard work. Hold the basket in one hand and place your baking parchment on top of it. With your other hand, hold the baking sheet over the dough and gently invert it all in one swift movement. Then just lift away the basket.

Spelt batons

You may have heard the words 'starter' or 'sponge' in relation to breadmaking – but what does it mean? It's basically a two-step process for making bread. The starter is made the day before you want to make the bread and left to ferment for between 12 and 24 hours. Get ready for a heady blast of yeast from the sponge mix when you uncover it – it is simply magical. Using a sponge in breadmaking will give you an amazing complexity of flavour. The yeast in the starter activates, bubbles away and slowly feeds on the natural sugars in the flour. This produces a tangy, slightly sour taste, hence the term 'sourdough'. I suppose a starter is a quick and easy way to make a form of sourdough without the need to keep a long-term sourdough starter. Here, the starter is made from spelt flour, which has a fantastic nutty taste.

Try this recipe for some fantastic crisp batons that go extremely well with my Paella (page 240).

MAKES 6 BATONS

Time required: 40 minutes preparation and two proves

Baking time: 20–25 minutes

Optimum oven position and setting: centre and no fan, with a baking stone

Essential equipment:
Two baking sheets; mine are aluminium and measure 38 x 32cm. Line with non-stick baking parchment
A couple of large bags to put the baking sheets into for proving

INGREDIENTS
350g strong white bread flour
1 tbsp extra-virgin olive oil
7g instant yeast
1 tsp fine salt
160ml water
a little rapeseed oil for greasing the proving bowl

For the sponge
150g spelt flour
½ tsp instant yeast
150ml cool water

METHOD

First make the sponge. Put the flour and yeast in a bowl and gradually add the water, stirring all the time. Give it a really good mix and then cover with clingfilm. Leave at room temperature for up to 24 hours.

To make the dough, put the flour, olive oil, yeast and salt in a large bowl. When adding the yeast and salt, place them at opposite sides of the bowl. Add the sponge mix, then add two-thirds of the water and begin to mix it all together with your fingers – or use a kitchen mixer with a dough hook. Add more water gradually until all the dry ingredients are picked up and you have a soft dough. You may not need all of the water.

Tip the mixture out onto a clean surface and knead it for 10 minutes. You'll work through the wet stage and eventually end up with a smooth, soft, silky dough. If you are using a kitchen mixer, knead it for about 6 minutes.

Lightly oil a large bowl and place the dough in it. Cover it with clingfilm or a shower cap and leave it on one side until doubled in size, about 1 hour, but it'll be fine for 2 hours.

When the dough has proved, tip it out onto a lightly floured surface (I use rice flour). Fold the dough over on itself a few times to knock it back. Weigh the dough and then divide it into six equal pieces.

Roll each piece of dough into a ball by making a cage shape with your hand and applying a gentle rolling pressure. Roll each ball of dough into a sausage shape tapering down to pointed ends, about 18cm long.

Line the baking sheets with non-stick baking parchment. Place three batons on each of the baking sheets, spacing them so they don't touch. Place each baking sheet inside a large bag to prove. Make sure the bag doesn't touch the dough. Prove again for about another hour, until doubled in size.

Preheat the oven to 200°C fan/220°C/390°F/gas 7. Place an empty roasting tin on the oven floor.

When the batons have doubled in size, take them out of the bags and use a sharp knife to make a lengthways slash about 2mm deep in the top of each one.

Bake each batch of three separately. Place one of the baking sheets in the centre of the oven and carefully pour about 150ml of boiling water into the roasting tin to create steam. Quickly close the oven door. Bake for 20–25 minutes. The batons should be a deep golden colour and sound hollow when tapped. You can test if they are baked to perfection by using a temperature probe: the centre of the rolls should be just over 90°C/195°F. Place on a wire rack to cool.

Spicy bread bowls

These bread bowls are a real showstopper for dinner parties. You can make large ones to use for a main course such as chilli con carne or a delicious thick stew, or smaller ones to use with a first-course soup. The outsides are super crisp, but once you cut into them you will find a soft fragrant crumb. Try them with my soup on page 74.

MAKES 4 LARGE OR 6 SMALL BOWLS

Time required: 30 minutes preparation and two proves

Baking time:
20–25 minutes, plus cooling

Optimum oven position and setting: centre and no fan, with a baking stone

Essential equipment:
Enamelled metal bowls for moulds. For large bread bowls: a bottom diameter of 90mm, top diameter of 150mm and 70mm high. For the smaller bowls: a bottom diameter of 85mm, top diameter of 120mm and 60mm high.
A baking sheet; mine is aluminium and measures 38 x 32cm
A large bag to put the baking sheet into for proving

INGREDIENTS

650g strong white bread flour
12g instant yeast
1 tsp fine salt
2 tsp sweet smoked paprika
pinch of chilli flakes
1 tsp garlic powder
1 tsp dried oregano
½ tsp freshly ground black pepper
1 tbsp extra-virgin olive oil
380ml cool water
rapeseed oil for greasing

METHOD

Place all the dry ingredients in a large bowl. When adding the yeast and salt, place them at opposite sides of the bowl. Add the olive oil and two-thirds of the water and begin to mix it all together with your fingers – or use a kitchen mixer with a dough hook. Add more water gradually until all the dry ingredients are picked up and you have a soft dough. You may not need all the water.

Tip the mixture out onto a clean surface and knead it for about 10 minutes. You will work through the initial wet stage and eventually end up with a smooth, soft, silky dough. If you are using a kitchen mixer, knead it for about 6 minutes.

Lightly oil a large bowl and place the dough in it. Cover it with clingfilm or a shower cap and leave it on one side until doubled in size. Depending on your room temperature, this can take 1 hour, but it'll be fine for 2 hours.

Grease each enamel bowl with a generous teaspoon of rapeseed oil. The oil stops the dough sticking to the bowl and also fries the outside slightly, giving a great flavour as well as robustness to hold the filling.

When the dough has proved, tip it out onto a lightly floured surface (I use rice flour). Fold the dough over on itself a few times to knock it back, then weigh it and divide it into four or six equal pieces.

If making the large bread bowls, form each piece of dough into a smooth round cob by repeatedly turning it on your lightly floured surface while constantly tucking it under itself, using your hands. This will give you a

tight, smooth top. Place each piece in an oiled enamel bowl.

If making the smaller bread bowls, roll each piece of dough by making a cage shape with your hand and applying a gentle rolling pressure. Place each piece in an oiled enamel bowl.

Put all the bowls on a baking sheet and put it inside a large bag to prove. Make sure the bag doesn't touch the dough. Leave it on one side until the dough in each bowl has doubled in size, about 1 hour.

Preheat the oven to 200°C fan/220°C/390°F/gas 7. Place an empty roasting tin on the oven floor.

Place the bowls on the baking sheet on the shelf in the oven. Carefully pour about 150ml of boiling water into the roasting tin to create steam, then quickly close the oven door. Bake for 20–25 minutes until deep golden and well risen. To check for perfection, use a temperature probe: the centre of the bowls should be just over 90°C/195°F.

Leave the bread to cool in the enamel bowls for about 2 minutes and then they should come out quite easily. Place on a wire rack to cool for a minimum of 30 minutes.

Using a bread knife, cut the tops off and gently dig out the soft inner bread to make hollow bowls. Cut up the soft bread and fry in a little olive oil for amazing croutons. Just before serving, pop the bowls into a preheated oven 200°C fan/220°C/390°F/gas 7 for about 5 minutes to crisp them up.

Spicy carrot, parsnip & coriander soup

This soup complements the bread bowls on page 72 perfectly. Flavoured with toasted Indian spices, sweet carrots and parsnips, it's sure to be a hit. You can make it in advance, it keeps well in the fridge for a couple of days or freezes excellently.

SERVES 4–6

INGREDIENTS

1 tbsp garam masala
1 tsp ground cumin
½ tsp turmeric powder
2 tbsp olive oil
    (not extra virgin)
2 small onions, chopped
1 garlic clove, chopped
500g carrots, chopped into
    2cm pieces
350g parsnips, chopped into
    2cm pieces
2 litres chicken stock
50g fresh coriander,
    coarsely chopped, plus
    extra for serving
fine salt and freshly ground
    black pepper
natural yogurt for serving

METHOD

Place the garam masala, cumin and turmeric in a large pot over a medium heat and toast for a couple of minutes. Be careful not to burn them.

Add the olive oil, onions and garlic, and gently fry for about 5 minutes.

Add the carrots and parsnips to the pot along with the chicken stock and bring to the boil. Reduce the heat, cover and simmer for 40 minutes.

Add the fresh coriander and simmer for another 10 minutes.

Turn off the heat and blend the soup until smooth. I use a stick blender straight into the pot. Season with salt and pepper to taste.

Garnish each bowl of soup with a tablespoon of yogurt and a few fresh coriander leaves.

Cheshire cheese & onion rolls

Just because I live in Cheshire, that isn't the only reason I use my local cheese in these rolls. Cheshire cheese is incredibly creamy but at the same time really robust. When you cut through these rolls, you are greeted with chunks of the cheese, as they survive the baking process to complement the onion slices perfectly.

Great for sandwiches or to go with a starter, these rolls pack lots of flavour. Next time you have a barbecue, forget brioche buns and give these a go with a smear of mustard and a burger cushioned in the middle.

These rolls are a great introduction to the world of flavoured breads.

METHOD

Heat the butter and olive oil in a frying pan over a low heat, add the onion and sauté until just translucent. Place in a bowl to cool.

Next, make the dough. Place the flour, yeast, sugar, salt and pepper in a large bowl. When adding the yeast and salt, place them at opposite sides of the bowl. Tip in the cooled onion.

Add the boiling water to the milk to give you a warm liquid. Add two-thirds of the liquid to the flour mixture and begin to mix it all together with your fingers – or use a kitchen mixer with a dough hook. Add more liquid gradually, until all the dry ingredients are picked up and you have a soft dough. You may not need all of the liquid, and bear in mind the onion will release moisture as you knead.

Tip the dough out onto a clean surface and knead it for about 10 minutes. You will work through the initial wet stage and eventually end up with a smooth, soft, silky dough. If you are using a kitchen mixer, knead it for about 6 minutes.

Lightly oil a large bowl and place the dough in it. Cover it with clingfilm or a shower cap and leave it on one side until doubled in size. Depending on your room temperature, this can take 1 hour, but it's fine to leave it for 2 hours.

When the dough has proved, tip it out onto a lightly floured surface (I use rice flour). Flatten it out with your hands and tip on the cheese. Knead the dough gently until the cheese is well folded in. Weigh the dough and then divide it into 13 equal pieces.

Shape six pieces of dough into rolls by making a cage shape with your hand and applying a gentle rolling pressure. As you roll them, place them on one of the prepared baking sheets, spacing them apart so they don't touch. Repeat with the remaining seven pieces of dough and place them on the other baking sheet.

Place each baking sheet inside a large bag to prove. Make sure the bag doesn't touch the dough. Prove again for about another hour, until doubled in size.

While the rolls are proving, preheat the oven to 180°C fan/200°C/360°F/gas 6.

When the rolls have doubled in size, take them out of the bags and mist with water. Sprinkle each roll generously with sesame seeds. Bake in two batches, one sheet at a time.

Bake for 20 minutes. They should be golden and sound hollow when tapped. You can test if they are baked to perfection by using a temperature probe: the centre of one of the rolls should be just over 90°C/195°F. Place on a wire rack to cool.

MAKES 13 ROLLS

Time required: 60 minutes preparation and two proves

Baking time: 20 minutes

Optimum oven position and setting: centre and no fan, with a baking stone

Essential equipment:
Two baking sheets; mine are aluminium and measure 38 x 32cm. Line with non-stick baking parchment
A couple of large bags to put the baking sheets into for proving

INGREDIENTS

30g unsalted butter
1 tsp olive oil
1 large red onion, diced – you need about 250g
600g strong white bread flour
12g instant yeast
1 tbsp caster sugar
1 tsp fine salt
½ tsp freshly ground black pepper
90ml boiling water
220ml whole milk
rapeseed oil for greasing
150g Cheshire cheese, coarsely crumbled
2 tbsp sesame seeds

Tikka masala breadsticks

These breadsticks will blow your socks off. Fragrant and crispy, every now and then while eating them you hit a sultana for a sweet fruit burst. They are really easy to make and go brilliantly with...well anything. They are fantastic as a snack or on a buffet table. Get down to your local Indian store for the gram flour (also known as besan, or chickpea flour), golden sultanas and spices. I've also included an alternative for basil and Parmesan breadsticks using the same technique. Experiment with different flavours to develop your own unique breadsticks.

MAKES 20 STICKS

Time required: 30 minutes preparation and two proves

Baking time: 10–12 minutes

Optimum oven position and setting: centre and no fan, with a baking stone

Essential equipment:
Two baking sheets; mine are aluminium and measure 38 x 32cm. Line with non-stick baking parchment
Two large bags for proving

INGREDIENTS
300g strong white bread flour
40g gram flour
7g instant yeast
1 tsp fine salt
25g caster sugar
½ tsp turmeric powder
1 tsp ground cumin
1 tsp ground coriander
½ tsp garlic powder
1 tsp garam masala
½ tsp ground ginger
½ tsp cayenne pepper
pinch of ground black pepper
3 tbsp sesame seeds
2 tbsp extra-virgin olive oil
200ml cool water
rapeseed oil for greasing
60g golden sultanas
rice flour or fine semolina for dusting

METHOD

Place all the dry ingredients, including the spices and 1 tablespoon of the sesame seeds (leave the golden sultanas on one side for now) in a large bowl. When adding the yeast and salt, place them at opposite sides of the bowl.

Add the olive oil and two-thirds of the water to the flour mixture and begin to mix it all together with your fingers – or use a kitchen mixer with a dough hook. Add more water gradually until all the dry ingredients are picked up and you have a soft dough. You may not need all of the water.

Tip the mixture out onto a clean surface and knead it for about 10 minutes. You will work through the initial wet stage and eventually end up with smooth, soft, silky dough. If you are using a kitchen mixer, knead it for about 6 minutes.

Lightly oil a large bowl and place the dough in it. Cover with clingfilm or a shower cap and leave it on one side until doubled in size. Depending on your room temperature, this can take 1 hour, but it's fine to leave it for 2 hours.

Dust your work surface with rice flour or semolina and tip the dough out onto it. (Using semolina will add a slight crunch to your breadsticks.) Flatten the dough to a rough rectangle and spread the sultanas over it. Fold it over on itself several times to distribute them evenly throughout.

Dust your work surface with more rice flour or semolina and roll out the dough to a 28 x 20cm rectangle. Sprinkle the top of the dough with the remaining sesame seeds and use the rolling pin to gently press them into the dough.

Using a knife or bench scraper, cut the dough into 20 strips, 1cm wide, and place them on the prepared baking sheets. Alternatively, you can make the breadsticks a little more rustic by dividing the dough into 20 equal pieces and rolling them into thin sausage shapes, 28cm long. Cover them with a tea towel and leave them to prove for about 20 minutes until slightly puffed up.

While the breadsticks prove, preheat the oven to 200°C fan/220°C/390°F/gas 7.

Bake each tray of breadsticks separately for about 10–12 minutes. They should be a deep golden colour and crisp.

Place on wire racks to cool. Best eaten on the day of baking.

Variation
BASIL AND PARMESAN BREADSTICKS
Follow the same technique for this tasty alternative. Replace the gram flour with strong white bread flour and all the spices, sultanas and sesame seeds with 3 tsp dried basil, 2 tsp poppy seeds and 50g finely grated Parmesan cheese.

Garlic & Parmesan monkey bread

A sweet pull-apart bread, baked in a bundt tin, is known as a monkey bread. The last time I made one it got me thinking, would it be possible to make a savoury version? I started thinking Parmesan cheese with garlic and herbs, and this recipe was born.

This bread is best enjoyed warm from the oven, after it has cooled slightly in the tin. So bake it just before you need it. It's fantastic served with a bowl of your favourite pasta.

SERVES 10

Time required: 45 minutes preparation and two proves

Baking time: 30 minutes

Optimum oven position and setting: centre and fan, with a baking stone

Essential equipment: A 24cm diameter bundt tin

INGREDIENTS

140ml boiling water
200ml whole milk
500g strong white
    bread flour
10g instant yeast
1 tsp fine salt
1 tsp garlic powder
30g Parmesan cheese,
    finely grated
rapeseed oil for greasing

To prepare the bundt tin

50g unsalted butter, well
    softened
40g plain flour

For the topping

100g unsalted butter
4 garlic cloves, finely grated
½ tsp dried oregano
½ tsp dried basil
½ tsp dried parsley
¼ tsp fine salt
50g Parmesan cheese,
    finely grated

METHOD

Add the boiling water to the milk to give you a warm liquid.

Put the flour, yeast, salt, garlic powder and cheese in a large bowl. When adding the yeast and salt, place them at opposite sides of the bowl. Add two-thirds of the liquid and begin to mix it all together with your fingers – or use a kitchen mixer with a dough hook. Add more liquid gradually until all the dry ingredients are picked up and you have a soft dough. You may not need all the liquid.

Tip the dough out onto a clean surface and knead it for about 10 minutes. You will work through the initial wet stage and eventually end up with a smooth, soft, silky dough. If you are using a kitchen mixer, knead it for about 6 minutes.

Lightly oil a large bowl and place the dough in it. Cover it with clingfilm or a shower cap and leave it on one side until doubled in size. Depending on your room temperature, this can take 1 hour, but it's fine to leave it for 2 hours.

Prepare the bundt tin. Brush the butter all over the inside of the tin. Be generous and make sure every single bit is coated. Tip in the flour and move the tin around to coat every nook and cranny, then give the tin a good knock out to get rid of any excess. Set aside.

When the dough has proved, tip it out onto a lightly floured surface (I use rice flour).

While the dough is proving, prepare the topping. Melt the butter in a large bowl in a microwave, or a saucepan, and add the grated garlic, then add the herbs, salt and Parmesan and give it a good stir.

Weigh the dough and divide it into 2 equal pieces. Roll each piece into a long sausage shape and divide it into 14 equal pieces, then roll them into balls.

Dip each dough ball into the topping mixture and place in the prepared tin. Keep going until you have placed all 28 pieces evenly around the inside of the tin.

Place the tin inside a large bag to prove. Make sure the bag doesn't touch the dough. You could also use a shower cap over the tin.

While the bread proves, preheat the oven to 160°C fan/180°C/320°F/gas 4.

When the bread has proved, bake for 30 minutes. You can test if it is baked to perfection by using a temperature probe: the centre of the bread should be just over 90°C/195°F. Leave to cool in the tin for 10 minutes before turning out onto your serving plate.

If you like, you can drizzle over some extra melted butter and sprinkle grated Parmesan cheese on the top. This bread is best eaten warm.

Northern milk loaf with a Japanese Hokkaido twist

I'm a northerner through and through, and I still enjoy a round sandwich made with the famous Blackpool milk roll. Soft, rich and with a very white crumb, it was a huge part of my childhood. So here's my interpretation. It's not round, but I love the style of Japanese Hokkaido bread (another form of milk loaf) so I'm using their technique to shape this loaf. It's quite a wet mix, so it's easier to make in a kitchen mixer with a dough hook. However, with patience it can be made by hand too. A little warmed honey brushed on the top of this loaf while still warm gives it a fantastic glaze and hint of sweetness.

MAKES 1 LOAF

Time required: 30 minutes preparation and two proves

Baking time: 30–35 minutes, plus cooling

Optimum oven position and setting: centre and no fan, with a baking stone

Essential equipment:
A 900g/2lb loaf tin; the base of mine measures 95 x 195mm and the tin is 70mm high. Grease and line it with non-stick baking parchment

INGREDIENTS
250ml whole milk
450g strong white bread flour
10g instant yeast
25g runny honey, plus 2 tbsp for glazing
40g unsalted butter, melted
1 tsp fine salt
a little rapeseed oil for greasing the proving bowl

METHOD
Warm the milk in a saucepan or microwave to around 35°C/95°F.

Place the flour, yeast, honey, butter and salt in a large bowl. When adding the yeast and salt, place them at opposite sides of the bowl. Add two-thirds of the milk and begin to mix it all together with your fingers – or use a kitchen mixer with a dough hook. Add the rest of the milk gradually until all the dry ingredients are picked up and you have a soft dough.

Tip the mixture out onto a clean surface and knead it for about 10 minutes. You will work through the initial wet stage and eventually end up with a smooth, soft, silky dough. If you are using a kitchen mixer, knead it for about 8 minutes.

Lightly oil a large bowl and place the dough in it. Cover it with clingfilm or a shower cap and leave it on one side until doubled in size. Depending on your room temperature, this can take 1 hour, but it'll be fine for 2 hours.

When the dough has proved, tip it out onto a lightly floured surface (I use rice flour). Fold it over on itself a couple of times, then weigh it. Divide into three equal pieces.

Roll each piece into a 30cm sausage, then roll each one out to a 9 x 30cm rectangle. Roll up each rectangle like a Swiss roll, starting at a short side. Place the pieces next to each other in the prepared tin. Place the tin in a large bag to prove until the dough is level with the top of the loaf tin. Make sure the bag doesn't touch the dough.

While the loaf is proving, preheat the oven to 180°C fan/200°C/360°F/gas 6.

Bake for 30–35 minutes until golden brown. You can test if it is baked to perfection by using a temperature probe: the centre of the bread should be just over 90°C/195°F. Leave to cool in the tin for 5 minutes before placing on a wire rack.

Gently warm 2 tablespoons of honey in the microwave and then brush generously over the warm loaf for a fabulous glossy glaze.

TIP *When is dough proved?*
The first clue is that the dough will have doubled in size. If you gently prod it, it should spring back and the indent should vanish pretty quickly. This shows that the gluten strands are holding gas (produced by the yeast) yet are flexible enough to allow the gas to bounce back.

Spiral seed & honey loaf

When you cut through this loaf, you can't help falling in love with the spiral you will see. Give me a slice of this loaf toasted and drenched in butter and I'm in heaven. The honey balances the savoury saltiness of the seeds. Use your favourite mix of seeds; I use a mixture of roasted sunflower, pumpkin, sesame, rapeseed and golden linseeds.

MAKES 1 LOAF

Time required: 30 minutes preparation and two proves

Baking time: 45 minutes

Optimum oven position and setting: centre and no fan, with a baking stone

Essential equipment:
A 900g/2lb loaf tin;
   the base of mine measures
   95 x 195mm and the tin is
   70mm high. Grease and
   line it with non-stick
   baking parchment

INGREDIENTS
500g strong white
   bread flour
7g instant yeast
30g runny honey
1 tsp fine salt
300ml water
a little rapeseed oil for
   greasing the proving bowl

For the filling
100g mixed seeds
1 tsp runny honey

METHOD
To make the dough, place all the ingredients, except the water, in a large bowl. When adding the yeast and salt, place them at opposite sides of the bowl. Add two-thirds of the water and begin to mix it all together with your fingers – or use a kitchen mixer with a dough hook. Add more water gradually until all the dry ingredients are picked up and you have a soft dough. You may not need all of the water.

Tip the mixture out onto a clean surface and knead it for about 10 minutes. You will work through the initial wet stage and eventually end up with a smooth, soft, silky dough. If you are using a kitchen mixer, knead it for about 6 minutes.

Lightly oil a large bowl and place the dough in it. Cover it with clingfilm or a shower cap and leave it on one side until doubled in size. Depending on your room temperature, this can take 1 hour, but it's fine to leave it for 2 hours.

When the dough has proved, tip it out onto a lightly floured surface (I use rice flour). Without knocking it back, roll it out to a rectangle roughly 25 x 30cm. Sprinkle the mixed seeds evenly over the dough, apart from a 3cm strip along one long side. Drizzle 1 teaspoon of honey all over the seeds.

Roll the dough up like a Swiss roll and then tuck a little of the two ends underneath itself. Place this roll in your loaf tin and put it inside a large bag to prove. Make sure the bag doesn't touch the dough. Leave it on one side until the dough has doubled in size, about 1 hour.

While the loaf proves, preheat the oven to 200°C fan/220°C/390°F/gas 7.

When the loaf has risen, dust the top with a little flour, using a fine sieve. Next, use a very sharp knife to carefully make two parallel slashes about 2–3mm deep in the top of the loaf to control how it will grow during baking. Be gentle when making the cuts so as not to deflate the loaf.

Bake for 15 minutes, then turn the oven down to 170°C fan/190°C/340°F/gas 5 for a further 30 minutes. You can test if it is baked to perfection by using a temperature probe: the centre of the loaf should be just over 90°C/195°F.

Opposites attract rye rolls

If you want to try something completely different in the world of breadmaking then these are for you. Once you make them, you will want to make them again and again. Looking down the list of ingredients you are probably thinking, 'he's completely lost the plot!' That's how I felt when I put everything together, but when I tasted them I knew that my crazy chemistry experiment had come good. These will wow your taste buds and they look super complex, but the technique to the shaping is embarrassingly easy to achieve. Cut through one and you will see the most amazing marbling. I love to eat these with a starter or filled with a slice of roast beef, a few rocket leaves, a smear of mayonnaise and English mustard.

MAKES 12 ROLLS

Time required: 80 minutes preparation and two proves

Baking time: 20 minutes

Optimum oven position and setting: centre and no fan, with a baking stone

Essential equipment:
2 baking sheets; mine are aluminium and measure 38 x 32cm. Line with non-stick baking parchment
A couple of large bags to put the baking sheets into for proving

INGREDIENTS
For the pale dough
2 parsnips (you need 75g), finely grated
75g rye flour
210g strong white bread flour
5g instant yeast
25g soft unsalted butter
½ tsp fine salt
½ tsp soft brown sugar
1 tsp whole fennel seeds
32g runny honey
160ml tepid water

For the dark dough
2 carrots (you need 75g), finely grated
75g rye flour
210g strong white bread flour
5g instant yeast
25g soft unsalted butter
½ tsp fine salt
½ tsp soft brown sugar
1 tbsp unsweetened cocoa powder
1 tbsp instant coffee granules
¼ tsp ground cloves
¼ tsp freshly ground black pepper
32g runny honey
160ml tepid water
200ml rapeseed oil for oiling the proving bowls and shaping

For the topping
8 tbsp black sesame seeds
8 tbsp white sesame seeds

METHOD
First make the pale dough. Place all the ingredients in a large bowl, except for the water. When adding the yeast and salt, place them at opposite sides of the bowl. Add two-thirds of the water and begin to mix it all together with your fingers – or use a kitchen mixer with a dough hook. Add more water gradually until all the dry ingredients are picked up and you have a soft dough. You may not need all of the water as the parsnip will release moisture.

Tip the dough out onto a clean surface and knead it for about 10 minutes. You will work through the initial wet stage and eventually end up with a smooth, soft, silky dough. If you are using a kitchen mixer, knead it for about 8 minutes. This type of bread takes a little longer to knead due to the low gluten content of the rye flour.

Lightly oil a large bowl and place the dough in it. Cover it with clingfilm or a shower cap and leave it on one side until doubled in size. This dough will take a couple of hours to prove at room temperature. You can place it in a warm place to speed things up a little.

Make the dark dough in the same way. Place it in an oiled bowl and leave in the same place as the pale dough to prove.

While the dough is proving, prepare a cutting board, a very sharp paring knife and a rolling pin. (I have a cutting board with a 10cm circle marked on it that I use as a template for these rolls.) Lightly oil the cutting board and a work surface with rapeseed oil. Spread the sesame seeds on a large plate.

continues overleaf…

Once the doughs have proved, tip them out and gently knock each one back using your fingers.

Each roll is made with 40g of each dough. Divide the dough into 40g pieces and roll each one into a ball. On the oiled surface, roll out a piece of the pale dough to a circle about 10cm wide and place it on the oiled cutting board. Pull it to a slightly oval shape; it should be about 3mm thick. Do the same with a piece of the dark dough, then place it on top of the pale dough and pat it down gently to stick them together [see fig. 1].

Cut four slots within the dough circle (all the way through - see fig.2) and then roll up the dough into a sausage shape [fig. 3]. Roll in the sesame seeds. Place the roll on one of the baking sheets in a crescent shape [fig.4]. Repeat until you have 12 rolls (6 on each baking sheet).

Place each baking sheet in a large plastic bag and prove again for about another hour. Make sure the bag doesn't touch the dough.

While the rolls are proving, preheat the oven to 180°C fan/ 200°C/360°F/gas 6.

When the rolls have doubled in size, bake one tray at a time for about 20 minutes until a dark golden colour. You can test if the rolls are baked to perfection by using a temperature probe: the centre should be just over 90°C/195°F. Place on a wire rack to cool.

TIP *Fast proving and slow proving*

Dough will prove quite happily at room temperature. The temperature dictates how long the prove takes. On average, standard strong bread flour dough will prove in 1 hour. Yeast can be made to work a little quicker by giving it a heat boost. If I'm in a rush, or am proving dough that usually takes a little longer, such as rye, the easiest way to give it a boost is to warm the liquid you are using to around 35°C/95°F. Take care not to go too far over that temperature as you could kill the yeast. Other ways to fast-prove dough include placing it in the airing cupboard, near a radiator or in your oven with the light turned on.

There is a sacrifice, though, because slow proving improves flavour. You can use this to your advantage and make the whole affair of making bread a lot easier. Make your dough the day before you want to bake the bread, place it in a covered oiled bowl and pop it in the fridge. It will live there quite happily for up to 24 hours and double in size. I do this all the time; it means you can have dough on hand to use when you are ready and end up with a massively improved flavour.

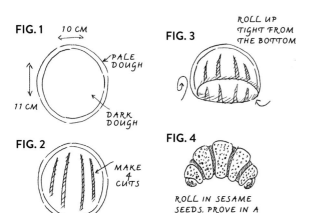

FIG. 1
10 CM
PALE DOUGH
11 CM
DARK DOUGH

FIG. 2
MAKE 4 CUTS

FIG. 3
ROLL UP TIGHT FROM THE BOTTOM

FIG. 4
ROLL IN SESAME SEEDS. PROVE IN A CRESCENT SHAPE

Ale focaccia

I'm going to take away the mystery of this bread. This slant on a traditional focaccia really is amazing. Made with real ale, I don't think I'll ever use just water again. The tangy, yeasty bread complements the saltiness of the olives and other toppings perfectly. Feel free to experiment with different toppings to find your favourite combination.

METHOD

Put the flour, olive oil, yeast, salt, pepper and about two-thirds of the ale in your mixer bowl and mix using the dough hook at a medium speed. As the dough comes together, add the rest of the ale and continue to mix for about 10 minutes. Eventually the dough will come together as the gluten builds and becomes really elastic.

Prepare the large plastic container by pouring in 2 tablespoons of olive oil and spreading it around. Tip the dough into the container and spread it out a little. Put the lid on and leave it at room temperature until it at least doubles in size. I usually leave it for about 1½ hours.

While the dough is proving, flour your work surface really well (I use a mixture of flour and fine semolina).

Tip your dough out gently onto the floured surface and then flour the top of the dough. Cut the dough in half with a bench scraper or knife and gently lift each half into its own prepared tin. Now gently press the dough out in each tin so it covers the base entirely. Brush the top of the dough with olive oil to prevent it drying out and leave to rise for about 40 minutes.

Press the olives, evenly spaced apart, into one of the pieces of dough. Make some indents with your fingers into the second piece of dough and sprinkle with chilli flakes, dried oregano, slices of red onion and sea salt flakes. Leave to prove at room temperature for about another 30 minutes.

While the dough proves, preheat the oven to 200°C fan/ 220°C/390°F/gas 7.

Place both tins of dough in the hot oven and bake for about 20–25 minutes until golden. Leave to cool in the tins for 5 minutes. Best eaten warm, with a drizzle of olive oil.

MAKES 2 FOCACCIA

Time required: 30 minutes preparation and two proves

Baking time: 20–25 minutes

Optimum oven position and setting: centre and no fan, with a baking stone

Essential equipment:
Two 33 x 23cm/13 x 9 inch baking tins – Swiss roll tins are perfect – lined with non-stick baking parchment
A 30 x 30cm plastic container with a tight-fitting lid for proving
A kitchen mixer fitted with a dough hook: this is a really wet dough

INGREDIENTS

500g strong white bread flour
30ml extra-virgin olive oil, plus 2 tbsp to grease the proving container
14g instant yeast
2 tsp fine salt
1 tsp freshly ground black pepper
400ml of your favourite real ale (I used Robinsons Trooper from my local Stockport brewery)
fine semolina for dusting

Topping 1
extra-virgin olive oil for brushing
200g pitted olives, dried on kitchen paper

Topping 2
extra-virgin olive oil for brushing
pinch of chilli flakes
pinch or two of dried oregano
1 red onion, finely sliced
pinch of coarse sea salt flakes

CHAPTER 3
Sweet doughs

1. Cherry & chocolate nougat babka loaf
Intertwined 3lb loaf tin babka with a crumble topping.

ALIEN BREAD!

2. Chocolate & nut clusters
A tear and share cluster loaf decorated with glacé cherries and kirsch icing drizzle.

3. Easy cranberry & maple brioche twists
How to make an overnight proved brioche dough and then create twists with a crème pâtissière and cranberry filling, topped with a maple glaze.

PERRY SAUCE

4. Pear & raisin kugelhopf with a perry sauce
A bundt-shaped kugelhopf with a pear cider sauce.

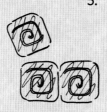

5. Cinnamon swirls with cream cheese frosting
Spectacular tray-baked cinnamon swirl cluster with a cream cheese drizzle. Alternatives also described for different fillings, such as peanut butter, biscuit spread or chocolate orange.

IRISH CREAM!

6. Doughnuts
Master the art of the filled doughnut with three flavour variations:
– Summer fruits jam
– Peanut butter and chocolate
– Irish cream cocktail

GREAT FUN TO MAKE!

7. Chocolate & hazelnut star bread
Step by step to create a tear-and-share sweet star bread.

Cherry & chocolate nougat babka loaf

The babka originates from Eastern Europe. My version is based on the Jewish variation that is traditionally twisted and filled with chocolate and cinnamon, with a streusel topping. The twisted dough is baked in a long loaf tin, which allows the dough to rise and still have enough room for the crumble topping. The babka is now very popular in North American bakeries in cities with large Jewish populations and is often taken as a gift to a dinner party.

MAKES 1 LOAF

Time required: 50 minutes preparation and two proves

Baking time: 55–60 minutes

Optimum oven position and setting: centre and no fan, with a baking stone

Essential equipment:
A kitchen mixer fitted with a dough hook
A 1.3kg/3lb loaf tin; the base of mine is 80 x 280mm and the tin is 70mm high. Grease and line it with non-stick baking parchment

INGREDIENTS
For the dough
500g strong white bread flour
10g instant yeast
1 tsp fine salt
50g caster sugar
1 medium egg
2 medium egg yolks
1 tbsp milk powder
1 tsp vanilla extract
200ml cool water
140g soft unsalted butter
rapeseed oil for greasing
1 medium egg, beaten, for glazing

For the filling
100g milk chocolate with nougat, coarsely chopped
30g soft unsalted butter
½ tsp fine salt
75g dried cherries, chopped

For the crumble topping
25g icing sugar
25g plain flour
25g cold unsalted butter
20g demerara sugar

METHOD
To make the dough, place the flour, yeast, salt, sugar, eggs, milk powder and vanilla in the mixer bowl. When adding the yeast and salt, place them at opposite sides of the bowl. Add two-thirds of the water and begin to mix it all together with the dough hook. Add more water gradually until all the dry ingredients are picked up and you have a soft dough. You may not need all the water. With the mixer still on, add the butter in thumb-size pieces until it is incorporated and the dough is smooth and shiny.

Lightly oil a large bowl and place the dough in it. Cover with clingfilm or a shower cap and leave it on one side until doubled in size (about 3–4 hours in a warm place).

While the dough proves, make the filling. Place the chocolate, butter and salt in a food processor and pulse to a thick paste.

When the dough has proved, tip it out onto a lightly floured surface (I use rice flour). Roll the dough out to a square about 26 x 26cm. Spread the chocolate paste evenly over the dough. Sprinkle the cherries evenly over the chocolate paste. Then roll the dough up tightly, like a Swiss roll, starting at the long edge nearest you. Cut the dough in half lengthways and twist the two lengths together. Place the twisted dough in the prepared tin. Place the tin inside a large bag to prove. Make sure the bag doesn't touch the dough. Prove again for about another hour until doubled in size.

Make the topping. Place the icing sugar and flour in a food processor and give it a quick pulse. Add the cold butter and pulse until the mixture resembles wet sand. Add the demerara sugar and pulse briefly to mix.

Preheat the oven to 180°C fan/200°C/ 360°F/gas 6. When the loaf has doubled in size, brush it lightly with the beaten egg and sprinkle over the crumble topping.

Bake for 55–60 minutes until deep golden. After 40 minutes, cover the loaf loosely with foil to stop the top browning too much. If you are baking it with a fan setting, it will bake more quickly. Test if it is baked to perfection by using a temperature probe: the centre of the loaf should be just over 90°C/195°F. Cool in the tin for 15 minutes, then place on a wire rack to cool fully.

Chocolate & nut clusters

As you have probably noticed by now, I like my bakes to look amazing. When I was developing this recipe a friend labelled it 'Alien from the planet Yum' due to the brash use of coloured glacé cherries and icing spirals. I prefer to call it a cluster tear and share loaf. Lots of small dough balls, packed with chocolate chips, each with a surprise crunchy nut inside. Topped with jewel-like glacé cherries and a spiral of kirsch-flavoured icing, I suppose it does have an air of some crazy alien from a 1970s sci-fi show. Have a look and decide for yourself.

The coloured glacé cherries I used on this bake are easily sourced online.

MAKES 1 'LOAF' OF 30 CLUSTERS

Time required: 40 minutes preparation and two proves

Baking time:
25–30 minutes, plus cooling

Optimum oven position and setting: centre and no fan, with a baking stone

Essential equipment:
A kitchen mixer fitted with a dough hook
A baking sheet; mine is aluminium and measures 38 x 32cm. Line with non-stick baking parchment
A large bag to put the baking sheet into for proving
For the spiral icing, you will need a disposable piping bag fitted with a 2mm plain round nozzle

INGREDIENTS

150ml whole milk
150ml boiling water
600g strong white bread flour
10g instant yeast
¼ tsp fine salt
75g caster sugar
1 medium egg, plus 1 egg, beaten, for glazing
finely grated zest of 2 oranges
100g soft unsalted butter
a little rapeseed oil for greasing the proving bowl
100g dark chocolate chips (fridge-cold)
10 whole blanched almonds
10 hazelnuts
10 pecan halves
15 glacé cherries, cut in half

For the icing
100g fondant icing sugar
1 tbsp kirsch or cherry brandy

METHOD

Put the milk in a heatproof jug and add the boiling water to give you a warm liquid.

Place the flour, yeast, salt, sugar, egg and orange zest in a mixing bowl. When adding the yeast and salt, place them at opposite sides of the bowl.

Add two-thirds of the liquid and begin to mix it all together with your fingers – or use a kitchen mixer with a dough hook. Add more liquid gradually until all the dry ingredients are picked up and you have a soft dough. You may not need all of the liquid. With the mixer still on, gradually add the butter in thumb-size pieces until it is all incorporated and the dough is smooth and shiny.

Lightly oil a large bowl and place the dough in it. Cover it with clingfilm or a shower cap and leave it on one side until doubled in size. This dough will take 2–3 hours to prove in a warm place.

When the dough has proved, tip it out onto a lightly floured surface. Using your hands, flatten it out to a large circle and place the cold chocolate chips on it. Fold the dough repeatedly in on itself to evenly distribute the chocolate chips. You can give it a few gentle kneads to achieve this.

Weigh your dough and then divide it into 3 equal pieces. Roll each piece into a sausage shape and divide it into 10 equal pieces. Roll each piece of dough into a ball by making a cage shape with your hand and applying a gentle rolling pressure. Flatten each ball slightly.

continues overleaf...

Place one whole almond onto a ball of dough and then bring up the sides of the dough to fully encase it and pinch them tightly closed. Gently roll the ball again and place it seam-side down on a lightly floured surface. Repeat with another 9 pieces of dough.

Repeat with the hazelnuts and pecans so you end up with 30 filled small dough balls.

Starting from the centre, place the dough balls on the lined baking sheet, leaving about 1cm space around each one. Place the baking sheet inside a large bag to prove. Make sure the bag doesn't touch the dough. Prove again for about another hour until doubled in size.

While the rolls are proving, preheat the oven to 160°C fan/180°C/320°F/gas 4.

When the dough balls have doubled in size, brush them lightly with the beaten egg and place a glacé cherry half on the top of each dough ball.

Bake for 25–30 minutes until golden. You can test if it is baked to perfection by using a temperature probe: the centre of one of the clusters should be just over 90°C/195°F. Place on a wire rack to cool completely.

Once the clusters have cooled, place the fondant icing sugar in a small bowl and add the kirsch. Mix to a smooth, really thick paste (add a little water if necessary). Place in a piping bag fitted with a 2mm round nozzle and pipe spirals around each cherry.

Easy cranberry & maple brioche twists

Brioche is quite different from other forms of bread. It's light, sweet and rich, thanks to the high egg and butter content. Traditionally the dough is very sticky and the first prove is in the fridge overnight. Not only does this improve flavour, but the cold firms up the dough so you can shape it. Speed is of the essence, though, as it soon starts to melt again. I've called my version an easy brioche as I've eliminated some of the peril. Its butter content is slightly lower, making it easier to handle and shape, but you will still get a great richness and crumb.

Make the dough and crème pâtissière filling the day before you want them. Both need to rest in the fridge overnight. The following day, make the twists and bake. Or you can pop them in the freezer straight after shaping. They will live there quite happily for up to 3 months. Defrost them at room temperature overnight and they will prove at the same time. Bake them first thing in the morning for a delicious breakfast treat.

If you are low on time, it's fine to use a good-quality ready-made custard instead of the crème pâtissière.

MAKES ABOUT 16 TWISTS

Time required: 75 minutes preparation and two proves over 2 days

Baking time: 30–40 minutes

Optimum oven position and setting: centre and no fan, with a baking stone

Essential equipment:
A kitchen mixer fitted with a dough hook
Two baking sheets; mine are aluminium and measure 38 x 32cm. Line with non-stick baking parchment
Two large bags to put the baking sheets into for proving

INGREDIENTS
For the dough
500g strong white bread flour
20g instant yeast
1 tsp fine salt
60g caster sugar
2 medium eggs
2 medium egg yolks
200ml whole milk
150g soft unsalted butter
a little rapeseed oil for greasing the proving bowl

For the filling
1 quantity (approx. 500g) of vanilla crème pâtissière (page 22)
finely grated zest of 2 oranges
100g dark chocolate chips
100g dried cranberries

For the maple syrup icing
30g unsalted butter
60ml maple syrup
125g icing sugar

METHOD

Make the crème pâtissière and stir in the orange zest just before covering it with clingfilm. Place in the fridge overnight.

To make the dough, place all the ingredients except the milk and butter in the bowl of a kitchen mixer fitted with a dough hook. When adding the yeast and salt, place them at opposite sides of the bowl. Add two-thirds of the milk and begin to mix it all together. Add more milk gradually until all the dry ingredients are picked up and you have a soft dough. You may not need all of the liquid. With the mixer still on, gradually add the butter in thumb-size pieces until it is all incorporated and the dough is smooth and shiny.

Lightly oil a large bowl and place the dough in it. Cover it with clingfilm or a shower cap and place it in the fridge overnight.

Take the dough from the fridge and divide it in two equal pieces. Roll out one piece to a rectangle approximately 25 x 50cm, with a long side nearest yourself. It should be about 4mm thick.

continues overleaf...

Whisk the crème pâtissière to loosen it and make it smooth. Using half of the crème pâtissière, spread an even layer over one half of the dough rectangle, using a palette knife. Sprinkle half of the chocolate chips and cranberries evenly over the crème pâtissière.

Fold over the uncovered half of the dough so no filling is visible. Cut the dough into 3cm wide strips. Twist one end of each strip four times and place on a prepared baking sheet. Repeat with the rest of the strips, leaving a 2cm gap between each one to allow for growth during proving and baking.

Make more twists using the other half of the dough and filling ingredients.

Place each baking sheet in a large bag to prove. Make sure the bag doesn't touch the dough. Prove again for about another hour until doubled in size.

While the twists are proving, preheat the oven to 180°C fan/200°C/360°F/gas 6.

Bake one tray of twists at a time for 15–20 minutes until golden. You can test if they are baked to perfection by using a temperature probe: the centre of a twist should be just over 90°C/195°F. Place on wire racks to cool fully.

While the twists are baking, make the icing. Place all the ingredients in a saucepan over a medium heat and stir continuously until melted and well combined. Set aside.

Place a tray under the wire racks to catch any drips and drizzle the warm icing over the warm twists. Eat warm or cold.

Pear & raisin kugelhopf with a perry sauce

The kugelhopf is a spectacular cake traditionally baked in a ceramic pan with a hole in the centre. Thought to originate in Austria, the kugelhopf is baked in various parts of Europe, with many countries having their own variations. Before the relatively modern invention of baking powder, all cakes were raised using yeast. This gives the kugelhopf a dense bready texture not dissimilar to the Italian panettone, but it's a lot quicker to make!

My variation has pears and raisins hidden inside the soft tender crumb, which is then doused in a thick pear cider sauce. Kugelhopf is traditionally eaten with a cup of coffee, and I'd recommend you do the same.

MAKES 1 CAKE

Time required: 30 minutes preparation and one prove

Baking time: 35–40 minutes

Optimum oven position and setting: centre and fan

Essential equipment:
A 10 cup/24cm/9½ inch diameter bundt tin
A kitchen mixer fitted with a paddle

INGREDIENTS

For the dough
200ml whole milk
25ml boiling water
85g soft unsalted butter
85g caster sugar
400g plain flour
seeds from 8 green cardamom pods, ground to a powder in a mortar and pestle
1 tsp fine salt
12g instant yeast
2 large eggs
3 conference pears (225g after peeling and coring)
75g seedless raisins

To prepare the bundt tin
50g unsalted butter, well softened
40g plain flour

For the sauce
50g unsalted butter
1 tsp vanilla extract
120g runny honey
100ml pear cider

METHOD

The first step to success with any bundt cake is preparation of the tin. Spending time doing this will ensure that the cake will pop out in one perfect piece. Brush the butter all over the inside of the bundt tin. Be generous, and make sure every single bit is coated. Tip in the flour and move the tin around to coat every nook and cranny, then give the tin a good knock out to get rid of excess flour. Set aside.

To make the dough, put the milk in a heatproof jug and add the boiling water to give you a warm liquid. In the kitchen mixer bowl, cream together the butter and caster sugar until pale and fluffy. Add the flour, ground cardamom, salt and yeast – make sure the yeast doesn't touch the salt. Add the warm milk mixture and the eggs, and mix using the paddle attachment, slowly at first to bring the mixture together, then increasing to medium speed. Continue to mix for 5 minutes.

Meanwhile, dice the pears into 1cm cubes.

The dough will be really sticky and stringy. Fold in the diced pears and raisins and place the dough evenly in the prepared tin. Cover with clingfilm or a shower cap and leave to prove until the dough has just reached the rim of the tin; this should take about 1 hour.

Preheat the oven to 170°C fan/190°C/340°F/gas 5. Then, when the cake has proved, bake for 35–40 minutes.

While the cake is baking, make the sauce. Put all the ingredients into a large shallow pan and bring to the boil. Boil until the sauce has reduced by about half and has become thick and glossy, with the consistency of double cream.

Check the cake after 30 minutes. It is ready when a skewer inserted in the centre comes out clean. The cake will have come away from the sides of the tin slightly.

Remove the cake from the oven and leave to cool in the tin for about 5 minutes. Turn out the cake onto your serving plate and leave to cool for another 5 minutes. Drizzle over the warm sauce.

Cinnamon swirls with cream cheese frosting

If I had to choose three recipes that I could only ever bake again, cinnamon swirls would definitely be one of them. Easy and fun to make, something amazing happens when cinnamon and cream cheese come together. These are a great tear and share bake, and the individual swirls are not too big.

MAKES 20 SWIRLS

Time required: 45 minutes preparation and two proves

Baking time: 20–25 minutes, plus cooling

Optimum oven position and setting: centre and no fan, with a baking stone

Essential equipment: A rectangular roasting tin; the tin I use is 35 x 25cm and 7cm high. Line it with non-stick baking parchment, taking time to line the sides

INGREDIENTS

For the dough
500g strong white
    bread flour
10g instant yeast
1 tsp fine salt
80g caster sugar
1 medium egg
300ml milk
40g soft unsalted butter
a little rapeseed oil for
    greasing the proving bowl

For the filling
75g soft unsalted butter
75g soft brown sugar

1 tbsp ground cinnamon
finely grated zest of 1 orange
200g sultanas (optional)

For the cream cheese drizzle
85g full-fat cream cheese
1 tbsp whole milk
80g icing sugar

METHOD

First make the dough. Place the flour, yeast, salt, sugar and egg in a large bowl. When adding the yeast and salt, place them at opposite sides of the bowl. Add two thirds of the milk and begin to mix it all together with your fingers – or use a kitchen mixer with a dough hook. Add the rest of the milk gradually until all the dry ingredients are picked up and you have a soft dough.

Mix for about 8 minutes. You will work through the wet stage and eventually end up with a smooth, soft, silky dough. While still mixing, gradually add the butter in small pieces until well incorporated. The dough should now be really smooth and glossy.

Lightly oil a large bowl and place the dough in it. Cover it with clingfilm or a shower cap and leave it on one side until doubled in size. Depending on your room temperature this can take 1 hour, but it'll be fine for 2 hours.

While the dough proves, make the filling. Warm the butter until it is just melted. Stir in the sugar, cinnamon and orange zest until smooth. Set aside.

When the dough has proved, tip it out onto a lightly floured surface (I use rice flour). Without knocking it back, roll the dough out to a rectangle roughly 50 x 25cm.

Using a large palette knife, spread the filling evenly all over the dough except for a 3cm strip along one long side. Sprinkle the sultanas evenly over the filling, if using them. Starting at the long side nearest you, roll up the dough like a Swiss roll.

Using a knife, cut the roll in half and then cut each half into 10 equal pieces. Place the swirls in the roasting tin in five rows of four each. Cover with clingfilm and leave to prove for 1 hour until the swirls have doubled in size.

While the swirls are proving, place your baking stone, if using, in the oven and preheat the oven to 180°C fan/200°C/350°F/gas 6.

Bake the swirls for 20–25 minutes until deep golden. You can test if they are baked to perfection by using a temperature probe: the centre of one of the rolls should be just over 90°C/195°F. Leave to cool in the tin for 15 minutes, then remove and leave to cool completely on a wire rack.

To make the cream cheese drizzle, put all the ingredients in a bowl and whisk well until smooth and runny. Spoon the cream cheese frosting into a disposable piping bag – or use a spoon – and drizzle all over the cooled swirls in diagonal lines.

TIP *Quick and easy fillings*

There are some great spreads available in the shops, so why not try them as an alternative filling in these swirls?

My favourite is the smooth cinnamon biscuit spread. Totally addictive stuff. Take 200g and place it in a heatproof bowl. Once you have your dough rolled out to a rectangle, warm the spread very gently in a microwave; it will become very runny. Spread it evenly over the dough and sprinkle over the sultanas. Roll up the dough and follow the rest of the recipe.

You could also try chocolate hazelnut spread, either on its own or dotted with peanut butter or a favourite jam.

Doughnuts

It's really hard to beat a homemade doughnut. They are amazing and really versatile. I must admit, I'm a jam doughnut man myself, but feel free to experiment with different fillings and toppings. Here, in their simplest form, they are rolled in sugar. If you like, you could add a little spice, such as cinnamon. Or you can go to town with different glazes, decorations and sprinkles. I've suggested some fun ideas on the following pages.

MAKES ABOUT 18 ROUND DOUGHNUTS

Time required: 60 minutes preparation and two proves

Frying time: 30–60 minutes

Essential equipment:
A kitchen mixer fitted with a dough hook
Two baking sheets; mine are aluminium and measure 38 x 32cm
A couple of large bags to put the baking sheets into for proving
A deep fat fryer filled with sunflower oil (see tip on page 103)

INGREDIENTS
100ml boiling water
150ml whole milk
500g strong white bread flour, plus extra (or rice flour) for dusting
14g instant yeast
1 tsp fine salt
2 medium eggs
60g caster sugar, plus 200g caster sugar for coating
60g soft unsalted butter
a little rapeseed oil for greasing the proving bowl

METHOD

Add the boiling water to the milk to give you a warm liquid.

Place the flour, yeast, salt, eggs and 60g of caster sugar in the bowl of a kitchen mixer fitted with a dough hook. When adding the yeast and salt, place them at opposite sides of the bowl. Add two-thirds of the liquid and begin to mix it all together. Add more liquid gradually until all the dry ingredients are picked up and you have a soft dough. You may not need all of the liquid.

Mix for about 8 minutes. You will work through the initial wet stage and eventually end up with a smooth, soft, silky dough. With the mixer still on, gradually add the butter in thumb-size pieces until it is all incorporated and the dough is smooth and shiny.

Lightly oil a large bowl and place the dough in it. Cover it with clingfilm or a shower cap and leave it on one side until doubled in size. Depending on your room temperature, this can take 1 hour, but it's fine to leave it for 2 hours.

Dust two baking sheets really well with flour or rice flour. Also dust your work surface and tip the proved dough out onto it. Fold the dough over on itself several times to knock the air out of it.

Using your scales, divide your dough into 50g pieces. Roll each piece of dough by making a cage shape with your hand and applying a gentle rolling pressure. This will give you smooth, taut buns. Flatten them ever so slightly and place them on the prepared baking sheets, spacing them apart so they don't touch. Place each baking sheet inside a large bag to prove. Make sure the bag doesn't touch the dough. Prove again for about 45–60 minutes until just doubled in size.

When the doughnuts are ready, heat the oil in your deep fat fryer to 160°C/320°F. Make sure the fryer is at this temperature all the time. If the oil is too cold, the doughnuts will be greasy; too hot and they'll be cooked on the outside but raw inside.

Using a thin, floured fish slice, spatula or scraper, slide it under each doughnut – you want to avoid deflating the doughnut – and gently place it in the fryer. Fry two or three at a time, making sure not to overcrowd and cool the fryer. The doughnuts will puff up. Fry them for 2–3 minutes on each side. They will end up with the distinctive white stripe around each one. You can test if they are fried to perfection by using a temperature probe: check the centre of one of the doughnuts is just over 90°C/195°F. When ready, lift them out of the fat with a slotted spoon and drain them on kitchen paper.

While still warm, roll them in a bowl filled with caster sugar (don't do this if you are making the peanut butter and chocolate flavoured versions). If you are going to fill them, place them on wire racks to cool completely before filling. You don't have to fill them – they are delicious as is!

Summer fruits jam doughnuts

Simple and classic, here is my take on the traditional jam doughnut. In its purest essence, it's just bread and jam – what's not to like? Feel free to choose your own combination of soft fruits for the jam.

METHOD

Make a batch of doughnuts and coat them in caster sugar. Leave them to cool.

To make the jam, purée all the fruits in a blender or food processor and then follow the instructions on page 26. I usually pour the jam into a large roasting tin to allow it to cool and set quickly.

When the jam is cold, place it in the piping bag.

Make a hole in the side of each doughnut, using a thin knife to pierce into the centre of the doughnut.

Pipe 30g of jam into each doughnut. To achieve this, weigh each doughnut and then fill it, weighing it as necessary until it is 30g heavier.

MAKES ABOUT 18 ROUND DOUGHNUTS

Time required: 90 minutes preparation and two proves, plus making the jam and filling the doughnuts

Frying time: 30–60 minutes

Essential equipment:
A sugar/jam thermometer
A piping bag fitted with a
    6mm filling nozzle

INGREDIENTS

1 batch of doughnuts
    (page 102)

Summer fruits jam
100g fresh strawberries
100g fresh raspberries
100g fresh blueberries
300g jam sugar
2 tbsp lemon juice
10g unsalted butter

TIP

If you're a doughnut fan, I really can't recommend enough that you invest in an electric deep fat fryer for both consistency and safety. The doughnuts need to be fried at a specific temperature and an electric fryer will achieve that for you.

Peanut butter & chocolate doughnuts

Peanut butter and chocolate is one of the greatest flavour combinations to come out of the United States. One of my missions in life was to discover a way of making peanut butter into a filling that can be used in a variety of bakes without gluing your mouth together. So I came up with a peanut butter crème pâtissière. It works incredibly well.

These doughnuts are filled with the peanut butter crème pâtissière and then dipped in warm chocolate before being finished with a sprinkle of salted peanuts and some sea salt flakes. Be sure to make the peanut butter crème pâtissière at least a few hours before you need it so it has time to cool and set.

MAKES ABOUT 18 ROUND DOUGHNUTS

Time required: 2 hours preparation and two proves, plus making the peanut butter crème pâtissière, filling and coating the doughnuts

Frying time: 30–60 minutes

Essential equipment:
A disposable piping bag fitted with a 6mm filling nozzle
A temperature probe

INGREDIENTS
1 batch of doughnuts (page 102)
1 quantity of peanut butter crème pâtissière (page 22)
75g salted peanuts
250g dark chocolate, coarsely chopped
2 tsp coarse sea salt flakes

METHOD
Ideally, make the crème pâtissière the day before you need it. Cover with clingfilm and place in the fridge overnight.

Make a batch of doughnuts, but don't coat them in caster sugar. Leave them to cool.

Make a hole in the side of each doughnut, using a thin knife to pierce into the centre of the doughnut.

Whisk the cold peanut butter crème pâtissière until fluffy and place in the piping bag. Pipe 45g of crème pat into each doughnut. To achieve this, weigh each doughnut and then fill it, weighing it as necessary until it is 45g heavier.

Put the peanuts into a food-safe bag and hit them with a rolling pin to break them up slightly.

Put the chocolate in a heatproof bowl placed over a saucepan of simmering water until melted. Make sure the water doesn't touch the bottom of the bowl. Alternatively, melt it in a microwave on low. Remove from the heat and leave to cool to 40°C/104°F. The reason for this crucial temperature is that the chocolate won't drip down the sides of the doughnuts after they have been dipped in it. You can place the bowl over a saucepan filled with warm water to keep it at the ideal temperature. Dip the top of each doughnut into the chocolate and then sprinkle over some of the peanuts and a few sea salt flakes.

Irish cream cocktail doughnuts

A certain very famous baking judge really liked these. So finally here is my most requested recipe – for these adult cocktail doughnuts. Yes, it's the ones with the Irish cream-filled straws sticking out of the tops! Serve them in cocktail glasses for that extra bit of fun.

MAKES ABOUT 18 ROUND DOUGHNUTS

Time required: 2 hours preparation and two proves, plus filling and glazing

Frying time: 30–60 minutes

Essential equipment:
A disposable piping bag fitted with a filling nozzle

INGREDIENTS

1 batch of doughnuts (page 102), made with 2 tbsp instant coffee granules

For the filling
650ml double cream
140ml Irish cream liqueur
50ml Kahlua liqueur

For the glaze
1 tsp instant coffee granules
1 tsp unsweetened cocoa powder
2 tbsp boiling water
140g full-fat soft cream cheese
140g icing sugar
2 tsp vanilla extract
4 tbsp whole-fat milk (if necessary)

50g dark chocolate (70% cocoa solids), finely grated
50g white chocolate, finely grated

For the filled straws
18 large straws (mine are 1cm diameter), cut to 14cm long
250ml Irish cream liqueur

METHOD

When making the doughnut dough, dissolve 2 tablespoons of coffee granules in the boiling water before adding to the milk.

Make a batch of doughnuts, but don't coat them in caster sugar. Leave them to cool.

Make a hole in the top of each doughnut, using a thin knife to pierce into the centre of the doughnut.

To make the filling, put the cream in a large bowl and whisk until soft peaks form. Add both liqueurs and whisk until just stiff. Place in the piping bag. Pipe 40g of filling into each doughnut. To achieve this, weigh each doughnut and then fill it, weighing it as necessary until it is 40g heavier.

To make the glaze, put the coffee, cocoa, boiling water, cream cheese, icing sugar and vanilla into a saucepan over a low heat, stirring all the time until the ingredients are well incorporated. The glaze should be runny enough to dip into without it running down the sides of the doughnuts. Add a little of the milk to thin it if necessary, or add a little more icing sugar if it is too thin. Dip the top of each doughnut into the glaze and then sprinkle a little of each chocolate onto the glaze.

Finally, block the bottom of each straw by piping a little of the leftover filling into it. Stick the straws into the doughnuts, blocked end first, with about 10cm sticking out of the top. Fill each straw to the top with Irish cream – I use a pipette to fill them. Go the extra mile and serve these doughnuts in cocktail glasses!

Chocolate hazelnut star bread

A stunning, delicious chocolate and hazelnut tear and share loaf. If you don't have a jar of chocolate hazelnut spread handy, you could use jam or marmalade. You can even make a savoury version with a pesto and feta cheese filling. In fact, you can fill it with anything you like as long as it's not too wet. It looks complicated but is actually very easy to do. I would usually make the dough and prove it overnight in the fridge for improved flavour, before finishing the loaf the next day. But you can make it all in one day if you prefer.

MAKES 1 STAR BREAD

Time required: 60 minutes preparation and two proves

Baking time: 20–25 minutes

Optimum oven position and setting: centre and no fan, with a baking stone

Essential equipment:
A kitchen mixer fitted with a
   dough hook
A baking sheet; mine is
   aluminium and measures
   38 x 32cm.
Non-stick baking parchment
A large bag to put the baking
   sheet into for proving

INGREDIENTS

135ml boiling water
135ml whole milk
500g strong white
   bread flour
14g instant yeast
1 tsp fine salt
2 medium eggs
100g soft unsalted butter
rapeseed oil, for greasing
2 tbsp smooth apricot jam

For the filling

200g chocolate hazelnut
   spread
finely grated zest of 1 orange
75g chopped roasted
   hazelnuts

METHOD

Add the boiling water to the milk to give you a warm liquid. Place the flour, yeast, salt and eggs in the bowl of a kitchen mixer fitted with a dough hook. When adding the yeast and salt, place them at opposite sides of the bowl. Add two-thirds of the liquid and begin to mix it all together. Add more liquid gradually until all the dry ingredients are picked up and you have a soft dough. You may not need all of the liquid.

Mix for about 8 minutes. You will work through the wet stage and eventually end up with a smooth, soft, silky dough. With the mixer still on, gradually add the butter in thumb-size pieces until it is all incorporated and the dough is smooth and shiny.

Lightly oil a large bowl and place the dough in it. Cover it with clingfilm or a shower cap and leave it on one side until doubled in size. Depending on your room temperature, this can take 1 hour, but it'll be fine for 2 hours.

Find the largest round plate you have that will fit completely on your baking sheet.

When the dough has proved, tip it out onto a lightly floured surface (I use rice flour). Fold the dough over on itself several times to knock the air out of it. Divide the dough into two equal pieces. Roll out one half of the dough on a piece of non-stick baking parchment into a circle just a little larger than your plate. Place the plate on the dough and trim around it with a knife.

To make the filling, place the chocolate spread in a heatproof bowl. Warm it gently in a microwave to make it runny. Using a palette knife, spread it evenly over the dough, leaving about 1cm bare all around the edge. Sprinkle over the orange zest and 50g of the chopped hazelnuts. (You could also sprinkle any other finely chopped nuts or dried fruit of your choice.)

Roll out the other half of the dough on a lightly floured surface and trim to the same size circle. Carefully place it over the chocolate-covered dough and press to seal around the edges.

Get a small bowl with a diameter of about 12cm and make a light imprint in the centre of the dough circle. Using a sharp knife, cut 16 equally spaced slices up to the circle imprint. The easy way to do that is to cut four evenly spaced, then another four in between those and so on. Gently lift each slice, spin over twice and lay back down. This will give you the amazing pattern. Twisting in one direction only will give you the pattern depicted in the photograph on page 110. Twisting each alternate section in opposite directions will give you the pattern depicted on page 111.

Slide the whole thing onto the baking sheet. Place the baking sheet inside a large bag to prove. Make sure the bag doesn't touch the dough. Prove again for about an hour until doubled in size.

Preheat the oven to 200°C fan/220°C/ 390°F/gas 7. Place your rack just below the centre of the oven. Bake the bread for about 20–25 minutes until golden.

Warm the apricot jam and brush it over the hot bread to glaze it. Sprinkle some chopped hazelnuts in the centre circle of the loaf – use a pastry cutter to sprinkle into and get a perfect circle of nuts. Eat warm or cold.

CHAPTER 4

Snacks & slices

1. Mini honey & malt Loaves
Small sweet malt loaves, ideal for lunchboxes or a teatime treat.

BISCUIT BASE   JAM

2. Oat flapjacks
A traditional cake-type flapjack baked on a digestive and jam base topped with flaked almonds.

3. Coconut & cherry macaroon slices
A tray bake made from coconut and glacé cherries.

USE UP LEFTOVER INGREDIENTS

4. Jammy thumbprint amaretti
Italian amaretti thumbprint cookies baked with a generous spoonful of jam.

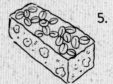

5. Fig and pecan parkin slices
Fig and pecan parkin slices. Not just for bonfire night.

6. Rosemary & thyme digestives
Rosemary and thyme biscuits to eat with cheese.

7. Spiced cinnamon crumpets
A traditional crumpet recipe livened up with a spice mix.

8. Cheese & paprika scones
Use up left-over cheese with this spicy scone recipe.

9. Chocolate chip scones
A twist on the classic.

10. Lemon & poppy seed madeleines
Zesty madeleines with poppy seeds.

Mini honey & malt loaves

A slice of the humble malt loaf has been enjoyed as a snack by many generations. Often associated with the 1950s, the malt loaf actually dates back to the late nineteenth century. Soft and squidgy, the debate continues as to whether it is a cake or bread. I decided to make mine the ultimate convenience food, baking them in mini loaf cases. Perfect for lunchboxes. Bake them low and slow and take them out of the oven before an inserted skewer comes out too clean, for that soft succulent centre. These get better after being stored in an airtight container for a day or so, if they last that long!

MAKES 10 MINI LOAVES

Time required: 20 minutes preparation

Baking time: 45–50 minutes

Optimum oven position and setting: bottom shelf and fan

Essential equipment:
10 mini loaf cases; the mini loaf cases I use measure 4 x 8cm at the base, and are 4cm high
A baking sheet; mine is aluminium and measures 38 x 32cm
A disposable piping bag

INGREDIENTS

175ml hot water
120g malt extract
85g runny honey
1 tbsp light muscovado sugar
100g raisins
100g sultanas
finely grated zest of 1 orange
1 tsp mixed spice
½ tsp salt
2 medium eggs, beaten
340g self-raising flour
½ tsp baking powder

METHOD

Preheat the oven to 140°C fan/160°C/285°F/gas 3.

Place the hot water, malt extract, honey and sugar in a large mixing bowl and stir to dissolve. Stir in the fruits, orange zest, mixed spice and salt. Add the eggs and stir until well combined. Sift in the flour and baking powder and fold until just combined.

Place the mixture in a piping bag and weigh the bag. Pipe an equal amount of mixture into each of the mini loaf cases: to do this, fill each case on a set of scales.

Place the loaf cases on the baking sheet and bake for 45–50 minutes. A skewer inserted into the centre should come out just a little bit sticky, not totally clean. Place on a wire rack to cool completely.

These will keep in an airtight container for up to 5 days, improving as time goes on.

Oat flapjacks

Whenever I make these, they always spark a debate. Most people argue that they aren't flapjacks, because they're nothing like the cereal-based bars we see in the shops nowadays. A flapjack should have a cake-like texture, made slightly heavier by the oats. A layer of jam and a biscuit base add flavour and another dimension. Trust me, once you have tried these, the flapjacks in the stores will seem like a poor relative.

MAKES 16 SLICES

Time required: 30 minutes preparation

Baking time:
30–40 minutes

Optimum oven position and setting: below centre and fan

Essential equipment:
A 20 x 30cm rectangular tin; I use a traybake tin, 5cm deep, with a loose bottom. Grease and line it with non-stick baking parchment

INGREDIENTS
For the biscuit base
160g digestive biscuits, crushed to fine crumbs
85g ground almonds
60g unsalted butter, melted
6 tbsp raspberry jam

For the flapjack mixture
60g unsalted butter
30g soft light brown sugar
80g caster sugar
70g golden syrup
90g rolled oats
60g oatmeal
110g plain flour
14g baking powder
2 medium eggs, beaten
½ tsp fine salt
250ml whole milk

METHOD

To make the base, put the biscuit crumbs in a bowl and stir in the ground almonds. Pour in the melted butter and mix really well. Tip the mixture into the prepared tin and press it over the base of the tin to make an even layer. Place in the fridge to set for about an hour.

Preheat the oven to 160°C fan/180°C/320°F/gas 4.

Gently spread the raspberry jam evenly over the biscuit base and set aside.

To make the flapjack mixture, put the butter, sugars and golden syrup into a large pan and gently heat until melted, stirring all the time. Stir in the rolled oats and oatmeal, followed by the rest of the ingredients. Stir it all together really well and then pour it over the biscuit base, spreading it around evenly using a spatula.

Bake for 30–40 minutes. After 30 minutes, test with a skewer inserted into the centre: the skewer should come out completely clean and the flapjack should have shrunk away from the sides slightly. It may need a few more minutes.

Leave to cool completely in the tin before removing and cutting into slices.

The slices will keep for 4 days in an airtight container.

Coconut & cherry macaroon slices

This is my sister-in-law Jane's signature bake. I think the recipe originates from the 1970s. These are really quick and easy to make, and perfect with a cup of tea.

METHOD

Preheat the oven to 160°C fan/180°C/320°F/gas 4.

Place the desiccated coconut in a large frying pan over a low heat and toast until just golden. Set aside to cool.

Place the egg whites in a large bowl and whisk until soft peaks form. Gradually add the sugar, whisking all the time, until the egg whites are thick and glossy. Using a large metal spoon, fold in the flour, cherries, grated chocolate and coconut, until well incorporated. Spread the mixture evenly in the prepared tin and bake for 45 minutes.

Place the tin on a wire rack to cool. Drizzle over the melted chocolate.

Place the whole tin in the fridge to set before cutting into slices.

The slices will keep for 5 days in an airtight container.

MAKES 16 SLICES

Time required: 20 minutes preparation

Baking time: 45 minutes

Optimum oven position and setting: below centre and fan

Essential equipment:
A 20 x 30cm rectangular tin; I use a traybake tin, 5cm deep, with a loose bottom. Grease and line it with non-stick baking parchment

INGREDIENTS

100g desiccated coconut
3 medium egg whites
110g caster sugar
35g plain flour
150g glacé cherries, cut into quarters
100g dark chocolate (70% cocoa), coarsely grated
50g dark chocolate (70% cocoa), melted

Jammy thumbprint amaretti

I inevitably end up with lots of jars with remnants of jams and marmalades. This is a great recipe for using them up and making something delicious at the same time. It's also a great way of using up any remnants of nuts or seeds I have for that extra crunch. Based on the incredible Italian amaretti biscuit, they are just fab.

MAKES 36 BISCUITS

Time required: 40 minutes preparation

Baking time: 15–20 minutes per batch

Optimum oven position and setting: centre and fan

Essential equipment:
Two baking sheets; mine are aluminium and measure 38 x 32cm. Line with non-stick baking parchment

INGREDIENTS

300g ground almonds
250g icing sugar, plus extra for dusting
85g plain flour
½ tsp fine salt
finely grated zest of 1 unwaxed lemon
3 tsp runny honey
1 tsp almond extract
3 medium egg whites
Your choice of chopped nuts or seeds to roll the biscuits in
Your choice of jams or marmalades for the thumbprints

METHOD

Preheat the oven to 160°C fan/180°C/ 320°F/gas 4.

Mix all the dry ingredients in a large mixing bowl. Add the honey, almond extract and egg whites, and mix to a smooth dough. Wrap the dough in clingfilm and leave in the fridge for at least an hour. It's really important you do this: the dough will firm up and become easy to handle.

Divide the dough into three equal pieces.

Dust your hands with icing sugar and roll each piece of dough into a sausage shape about 3cm thick. Roll it in your choice of chopped nuts or seeds. Try different nuts or seeds for each sausage. Cut each sausage into 12 equal discs. Dip the exposed sides of each disc in icing sugar.

Keep your hands dusted in icing sugar and place the discs on the prepared baking sheet, 2–3cm apart. Press your thumb into the centre of each one to make an indent. Fill the indent with ¼ teaspoon of jam or marmalade.

As soon as you have a full tray, bake for 15–20 minutes until golden and risen. Repeat until you have used up all the dough.

Leave them to cool on the baking sheets. They will become crisp as they cool.

Fig & pecan parkin slices

It seems a shame that parkin is associated with Bonfire Night and ignored for the rest of year. Well, I refuse to wait 12 months for it. Parkin is a rich cake that has many versions from all over the north of England. Thought to originate from the early 1700s, it's one of those great cakes that get better in the days after you bake it.

My version is a little different. I use lots of treacle for a deep rich flavour, and figs and pecan nuts to add an amazing crunch.

MAKES 16 SLICES

Time required: 30 minutes preparation

Baking time: 40–45 minutes

Optimum oven position and setting: below centre and fan

Essential equipment: A 20 x 30cm rectangular tin; I use a traybake tin, 5cm deep, with a loose bottom. Grease and line with non-stick baking parchment

INGREDIENTS

300ml of your favourite ale or beer
200g black treacle
250g golden syrup
225g plain flour
1 tsp bicarbonate of soda
3 tsp ground ginger
85g cold unsalted butter, cut into 1cm cubes
85g cold lard, cut into 1cm cubes
100g dried figs, coarsely chopped
100g pecan nuts, coarsely chopped
225g medium oatmeal
1 large egg, beaten
50g rolled oats for the topping

METHOD

Preheat the oven to 140°C fan/160°C/285°F/gas 3.

Place the ale, treacle and golden syrup in a large saucepan over a low heat and gently stir until the treacle has dissolved. Remove from the heat and set aside.

Place the flour, bicarbonate of soda, ginger, butter and lard in a food processor and pulse until it resembles breadcrumbs. Alternatively, rub them together using your fingers. Place them in a large mixing bowl and mix in the figs, nuts, oatmeal and egg to a stiff mixture.

Add the beer mixture and mix to a smooth consistency. Pour the mixture into the prepared tin and level the top with a spatula. Sprinkle the rolled oats evenly over the top.

Bake for 40–45 minutes. After 40 minutes, test the parkin with a skewer inserted into the centre: the skewer should come out completely clean and the cake should have shrunk away from the sides of the tin slightly. It may need a few more minutes.

Leave to cool in the tin for 10 minutes before placing on a wire rack to cool completely.

Cut into slices when cool. The slices will keep for up to 7 days in an airtight container.

Rosemary & thyme digestives

I'm a secret cheese and digestive eater, despite the fact they are traditionally dipped in tea. But I firmly believe the digestive biscuit has a place on the cheeseboard. This recipe will give you the perfect excuse to break with tradition and help my campaign. Give them a go and never look back.

MAKES ABOUT 24–30 BISCUITS

Time required:
40 minutes preparation

Baking time: 15–20 minutes

Optimum oven position and setting: centre and fan

Essential equipment:
A food processor fitted with a blade
Two baking sheets; mine are aluminium and measure 38 x 32cm. Line with non-stick baking parchment
A 7cm round cutter

INGREDIENTS

330g wholemeal flour
330g medium oatmeal
50g soft brown muscovado sugar
1½ tsp baking powder
½ tsp fine salt
½ tsp freshly ground black pepper
225g cold unsalted butter, cut into 1cm cubes
5 tbsp finely chopped fresh rosemary
2 tbsp finely chopped fresh thyme leaves
2 tbsp finely chopped fresh lemon thyme leaves
1 tsp cider vinegar
2 tbsp whole milk
1 tbsp coarse sea salt flakes
plain flour for dusting

METHOD

Preheat the oven to 160°C fan/180°C/320°F/gas 4.

Place the flour, oatmeal, sugar, baking powder, salt, pepper and butter in a food processor. Pulse until it resembles fine breadcrumbs.

Place the mixture into a large mixing bowl and add the rest of the ingredients. Mix together with your hands and knead until a really stiff dough comes together.

Divide the dough into three equal pieces and roll each piece out to a thickness of about 4mm on a very lightly floured surface.

Cut out the biscuits using a 7cm cutter, lift them with a palette knife, and place on the prepared baking sheets. Sprinkle a few sea salt flakes on each biscuit.

As soon as a baking sheet is full, bake for 15–20 minutes until deep golden and slightly risen. Repeat until you have used up all the dough.

Place on wire racks to cool. The biscuits will keep for 5 days in an airtight container.

TIP

Herbs on hand

I try to use fresh herbs whenever possible. An easy way of keeping a constant supply on hand is to freeze them. They freeze really well and I only pull out what I need. There's no need to defrost, as they are ready to use almost instantly.

Spiced cinnamon crumpets

Crumpets are the perfect comfort food. Just throw them in a toaster, and the hundreds of little holes are the perfect carrier for your favourite topping. They are incredibly easy to make, too. The batter is an all-in-one mix that can be made even quicker by whizzing it all in a food processor for a minute. Alternatively, give it a good old beating in a large mixing bowl to build up some of the gluten in the flour. This will ultimately give you the perfect texture.

MAKES ABOUT 12 CRUMPETS

Time required: 40 minutes preparation and one prove

Frying time: 25 minutes

Essential equipment:
Four metal crumpet rings
A large non-stick frying pan

INGREDIENTS
250ml whole milk
12g soft unsalted butter
1 tbsp caster sugar
1 tsp fine salt
250ml boiling water
75g plain flour
280g strong white bread flour
14g instant yeast
½ tsp bicarbonate of soda
½ tsp ground cinnamon
¼ tsp mixed spice
2 tbsp sunflower oil for frying

METHOD
Place the milk, butter, sugar and salt in a heatproof jug. Pour in the boiling water and stir until everything is dissolved.

Place both flours, the yeast, bicarbonate of soda, cinnamon and spice in the bowl of your food processor or a large mixing bowl.

Add the fluid and, if using a food processor, mix it all together for a minute. If using a bowl, mix it all with a large spoon for about 4 minutes.

Cover with clingfilm and place on one side for 45 minutes. The mixture will rise and be very lively. Pour it very gently into a large jug.

Place a non-stick frying pan over a low to medium heat. Grease the crumpet rings and frying pan a little with a brush or kitchen towel dipped in the oil. Place the rings in the frying pan and leave to heat up for a minute.

Slowly pour some of the crumpet mixture into each ring. Don't fill the ring more than halfway or you won't get the distinctive bubbled top. Cook for about 6–7 minutes until the holes in the top of the crumpet have formed and are starting to set.

Remove the rings; you may have to run a knife around the edge. Turn the crumpets over and fry for a further minute.

Place on a wire rack to cool. Continue until you have used up all of the batter. Eat warm or store in an airtight container and toast later.

Cheese & paprika scones

These scones pack a spicy, cheesy punch. They are fantastic warm, cut in half and slathered in butter. I use a combination of mature Cheddar and Manchego cheese – the Cheddar provides a strong cheese flavour, the Manchego gives creaminess – but you can use up other types of leftover cheese.

The key to great scones is to handle the mixture as little as possible. It should be wet and slightly sticky to ensure a short, crumbly texture and a good rise. A food processor fitted with a blade gives great results. However, you can use your fingers to rub together the dry ingredients and butter.

MAKES 15 SCONES

Time required: 20 minutes preparation

Baking time: 12–15 minutes

Optimum oven position and setting: centre and fan

Essential equipment:
A baking sheet; mine is aluminium and measures 38 x 32cm. Line with non-stick baking parchment
A 7cm round fluted cutter

INGREDIENTS

100g mature Cheddar cheese, grated
50g Manchego cheese, grated
200ml whole milk
1 medium egg, beaten
1 tsp vegetable oil
375g self-raising flour
1½ tsp baking powder
½ tsp fine salt
½ tsp freshly ground black pepper
½ tsp sweet (*dulce*) smoked paprika
¼ tsp English mustard powder
¼ tsp cayenne pepper
60g cold unsalted butter, cut into 1cm cubes

For the topping
1 medium egg, beaten
1 tbsp whole milk
50g mature Cheddar cheese, grated

METHOD

Preheat the oven to 200°C fan/220°C/390°F/gas 7.

Combine the two cheeses in a bowl and set aside. Whisk together the milk, egg and vegetable oil in a large jug. Set aside.

Put the flour, baking powder, salt, pepper and spices in your food processor and give it a few quick pulses to mix it all up. Add the butter and pulse again until the mixture resembles breadcrumbs.

Tip the mixture into a large bowl and mix in the cheeses. Don't overwork the mixture. Make a well in the centre and pour in the liquid. Using a fork, fold the mixture together to form a dough.

Tip the dough out onto a floured surface. Flour your hands and pat the dough flat to a thickness of about 2cm. Cut out 7cm rounds and place them upside down on the prepared baking sheet. Gently bring the trimmings together and cut out more rounds.

For the topping, beat together the egg and milk. Brush over the top of the scones and then sprinkle a little cheese on the top of each one. Try not to let any glaze run down the sides, as it can stop the scones rising.

Bake for 12–15 minutes until golden and risen. Place on a wire rack to cool.

These are best eaten on the day of baking. However, they freeze brilliantly. Defrost at room temperature, then pop them into a preheated oven for 5 minutes to warm and refresh them.

Chocolate chip scones

These sweet scones are great for any time of the day. Perfect as a grab-and-go breakfast snack, or cut one in half and fill it with your favourite spread, with a cup of coffee in the afternoon.

METHOD

Preheat the oven to 200°C fan/220°C/ 390°F/gas 7.

Whisk together the milk, egg, vegetable oil and orange extract in a large jug. Set aside.

Put the flour, salt, baking powder and orange zest in your food processor and give it a few quick pulses to mix it all up. Add the butter and pulse again until the mixture resembles breadcrumbs.

Tip the mixture into a large bowl and mix in the sugar and chocolate chips. Don't overwork the mixture. Make a well in the centre and pour in the liquid. Using a fork, fold the mixture together to form a dough.

Tip the dough out onto a floured surface. Flour your hands and pat the dough flat to a thickness of about 2cm. Cut out 7cm rounds and place them upside down on the prepared baking sheet. Gently bring the trimmings together and cut out more rounds.

Glaze the top of the scones with the egg and milk mixture. Try not to let any glaze run down the sides, as it can stop the scones rising.

Bake for 12–15 minutes until golden and risen. Place on a wire rack to cool.

These are best eaten on the day of baking. However, they freeze brilliantly. Defrost at room temperature, then pop them into a preheated oven for 5 minutes to warm and refresh them.

MAKES 12 SCONES

Time required: 20 minutes preparation

Baking time: 12–15 minutes

Optimum oven position and setting: centre and fan

Essential equipment:
A baking sheet; mine is aluminium and measures 38 x 32cm. Line with non-stick baking parchment
A 7cm round fluted cutter

INGREDIENTS

200ml whole milk
1 medium egg, beaten
1 tsp vegetable oil
1 tsp orange extract
375g self-raising flour
¼ tsp fine salt
1½ tsp baking powder
finely grated zest of 1 orange
60g cold unsalted butter, cut into 1cm cubes
40g caster sugar
75g dark chocolate chips
1 medium egg, beaten with 1 tbsp whole milk, for glazing

Lemon & poppy seed madeleines

One of the simplest and greatest cakes in the world, the madeleine originates from north-eastern France. It is traditionally baked in shell-shaped moulds, and these are easily available. The sponge is light, based on a genoise batter; this is where melted butter is folded into the mixture for a delicate, rich finish.

MAKES 12–16, DEPENDING ON YOUR MADELEINE TIN

Time required: 20 minutes preparation

Baking time: 10 minutes

Optimum oven position and setting: centre and fan

Essential equipment: A madeleine tin

INGREDIENTS

40g self-raising flour
40g plain flour
2 medium eggs
35g caster sugar
35g icing sugar, plus extra for dusting
1 tsp poppy seeds
1 tbsp lemon juice
finely grated zest of 1 unwaxed lemon
80g unsalted butter, melted

To prepare the madeleine tin
30g unsalted butter, melted
30g plain flour

METHOD

Preheat the oven to 180°C fan/200°C/360°F/gas 6. Prepare your madeleine tin. Brush it well with melted butter, then sprinkle the flour over it. Turn it upside down and tap it to knock out any excess flour.

Sift both flours together into a bowl.

In a clean bowl, whisk together the eggs and both sugars until pale and frothy. Mix in the flours, poppy seeds, lemon juice and lemon zest. Finally fold in the melted butter.

Pour a little of the mixture into each mould and bake for 10 minutes until risen and golden.

Tip the madeleines out and place on a wire rack to cool, shell side up. Dust with icing sugar to finish. These are best eaten within a day of baking.

CHAPTER 5
Tarts

1. Pecan & pistachio pie
My take on the American Thanksgiving classic.

TRY FEATHERED ICING

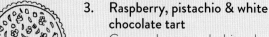

2. Bakewell tart
Traditional family-size Bakewell tart with an iced feathered top and glacé cherries. Variation also for a blueberry version.

GREAT AFTER DINNER DESSERT

3. Raspberry, pistachio & white chocolate tart
Cream cheese and white chocolate filled tart with fresh raspberries, topped with pistachios.

4. Caramelized orange & mango custard tart
Learn how to make the perfect smooth custard tart with confidence.

CHERRY BRANDY DRIZZLES

5. Sultana & Calvados custard tarts
Individual baked custard tarts with sultanas.

6 **Butterscotch meringue tart**
Deep filled butterscotch tart with
a flamed Italian meringue topping.

7. **Chocolate simnel tart**
A centrepiece long tart based on
the traditional Easter simnel cake

8. **Pumpkin pie**
Traditional American sweet
pumpkin pie.

9. **Chocolate cherry tart with cherry brandy drizzles**
A real centrepiece chocolate
pastry tart. Filled with a baked
mascarpone, chocolate and
macerated cherries filling. Each
individual slice comes with a pipette
of drizzling cherry brandy syrup.

10. **Orange caramel mini tarts**
Great after-dinner dessert. Mini
custard tarts with a crème caramel-
type filling and orange segments.

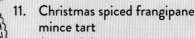

NO BLIND
BAKING!

11. **Christmas spiced frangipane mince tart**
A round shortcrust pastry tart
filled with sweet mincemeat
and a spiced almond frangipane.
Topped with lemon icing drizzle
and green and red glacé cherries.

12. **Aparagus & pancetta tart**
Showstopping long shortcrust
pastry tart.

13. **Tortilla tart**
The humble Spanish omelette
converted into a picnic tart.

14. **Cheese & onion flan**
My mother-in-law Rita's
legendary cheese and onion
flan. Great for a light dinner
or buffet meal.

Pecan & pistachio pie

The pecan pie is a firm Thanksgiving favourite in the United States. Originating in the South, there are now many variations from all parts of the country. This tart is about as indulgent as it gets, with a rich, nutty, syrup-based filling.

My version goes off piste a little. A dark corn syrup is traditionally used as the basis for the pie in the States, but I prefer golden syrup. A hint of lemon zest helps cut through the sweetness. I also add a handful of pistachio nuts for some variation in each mouthful. Take the time to lightly toast the nuts – it really makes a difference to the flavour.

This tart is best served warm and goes brilliantly with whipped cream or vanilla ice cream.

SERVES 8

Time required:
60 minutes preparation

Baking time:
30–40 minutes

Optimum oven position and setting: below centre and fan

Essential equipment:
A 23cm tart tin with a loose bottom; mine is 35mm deep – the extra height is really useful for a slightly deeper tart
A baking sheet; mine is aluminium and measures 38 x 32cm

INGREDIENTS

1 quantity of sweet shortcrust pastry (page 15), blind baked in a 23cm tart tin (page 16)
150g pecan nuts, coarsely chopped
50g pistachio nuts
200g soft light brown sugar
160ml golden syrup
30ml black treacle
2 tbsp bourbon whiskey
½ tsp fine salt
3 large eggs
1 tsp vanilla paste
finely grated zest of 1 unwaxed lemon

For the topping
25 perfect pecan nut halves

METHOD

Preheat the oven to 160°C fan/180°C/320°F/gas 4.

Place the chopped pecans and pistachios on a baking sheet and place in the oven for 5 minutes to toast them slightly. Remove and leave to cool.

Put the sugar, syrup, treacle, bourbon and salt in a large pan over a medium heat and bring to the boil for 3 minutes, stirring continuously. Set aside to cool for 20 minutes.

Whisk the eggs into the cooled syrup, followed by the vanilla paste and lemon zest. Stir in the pecans and pistachios and pour into the pastry case.

Arrange the perfect pecan nut halves gently on the filling around the edge.

Bake for 30–40 minutes. The tart is ready when the edges of the filling are set and there is a slight wobble in the centre.

Place on a wire rack and leave to cool in the tin slightly before placing on your presentation plate. Eat warm or cold.

Bakewell tart

The Bakewell tart got me into baking. I live fairly close to Bakewell in the Peak District and would frequently take a visit there to stock up on the famous tarts, as well as the lesser-known Bakewell pudding. My mission was to learn how to make it. The Bakewell tart is a fantastic tutor in the world of baking. It teaches you how to make and blind bake pastry (it doesn't matter if it's not perfect), how to make a cake-like frangipane filling and also the art of decoration. It's a great place to start as well as being totally delicious.

METHOD

Preheat the oven to 160°C fan/180°C/320°F/gas 4.

Spread the raspberry jam evenly over the pastry case – don't go right to the edge, but leave about 1cm jam-free all the way around.

To make the frangipane, cream together the butter and sugar until pale and fluffy; this takes about 5 minutes in a kitchen mixer fitted with a paddle, or a little longer with a hand mixer. Fold in the remaining ingredients and place the mixture in a disposable piping bag. Cut the end off the bag to make a hole about 12mm wide and pipe the mixture evenly into the pastry case over the jam layer. Smooth out gently using a palette knife or spatula.

Place the tart tin on a baking sheet and bake for 25–30 minutes until the filling is golden. Test with a skewer inserted into the centre: it should come out clean and the frangipane should be firm to the touch.

Place on a wire rack and leave to cool completely before removing the tart from the tin.

To make the topping, put the icing sugar in a mixing bowl with the almond extract. Stir while adding a little water until you have a thick, smooth fondant.

Place 2 tablespoons of the fondant in a small bowl and colour it bright red. Place in a disposable piping bag fitted with a 2mm plain round nozzle.

Pour the white fondant mixture into the tart tin until level with the top. Pipe parallel lines of red fondant on the tart and then drag a toothpick across the lines to create a feathered effect. Place a red glacé cherry in the centre.

SERVES 8

Time required: 60 minutes preparation

Baking time: 25–30 minutes

Optimum oven position and setting: centre and fan

Essential equipment:
A 23cm tart tin with a loose bottom; mine is 35mm deep – the extra height is really useful for a slightly deeper tart
A baking sheet; mine is aluminium and measures 38 x 32cm
A couple of disposable piping bags and a 2mm round piping nozzle

INGREDIENTS

1 quantity of sweet shortcrust pastry (page 15), blind baked in a 23cm tart tin (page 16)
2 tbsp raspberry jam

For the frangipane filling
75g unsalted butter
75g caster sugar
75g ground almonds
1 tbsp plain flour
1 tsp almond extract
finely grated zest of 1 unwaxed lemon
1 medium egg, beaten

For the topping
200g icing sugar
1 tsp almond extract
red food colouring gel
a red glacé cherry

Variation

BLUEBERRY BAKEWELL TART

Why not try a blueberry twist on the traditional Bakewell tart? Simply replace the raspberry jam with blueberry jam, and decorate the top with about 100g fresh blueberries gently placed on the icing.

Raspberry, pistachio & white chocolate tart

I first made this tart for a family Sunday dinner and it was an immediate hit. Hidden in the mascarpone and white chocolate filling are fresh raspberries for a hint of tartness. The tart is topped with chopped pistachios and fresh pomegranate seeds, but feel free to add fresh raspberries and some grated white chocolate too.

SERVES 12

Time required: 60 minutes preparation

Baking time: 25–30 minutes

Optimum oven position and setting: centre and fan

Essential equipment:
A 26cm tart tin with a loose bottom; mine is 30mm deep
A baking sheet; mine is aluminium and measures 38 x 32cm

INGREDIENTS

1 quantity of sweet shortcrust pastry (page 15), blind baked in a 26cm tart tin (page 16)
100g good-quality white chocolate, coarsely chopped
200ml double cream
300g mascarpone cheese
1½ tsp vanilla paste, or 2 tsp vanilla extract
3 medium eggs
250g fresh raspberries
½ fresh pomegranate
100g pistachios, coarsely chopped – or use slivered pistachios, which look amazing

METHOD

Preheat the oven to 160°C fan/180°C/320°F/gas 4.

Put the white chocolate in a heatproof bowl with the double cream and place over a saucepan of simmering water. Make sure the water doesn't touch the bottom of the bowl. Stir until the chocolate has melted.

Leave to cool for a couple of minutes, then add the mascarpone, vanilla and eggs, and whisk very lightly until combined. Try not to get air into the mixture.

Pour two-thirds of the mixture into the pastry case and then add the raspberries, distributing them evenly. Add the rest of the mixture until you get to within 3mm of the top. Make sure the raspberries are submerged.

Place the tart tin on a baking sheet and bake for 25–30 minutes until the filling feels firm in the centre and you start to see a little cracking around the edges.

Place on a wire rack and leave to cool completely before removing the tart from the tin.

Using a wooden spoon, hit the back of the halved pomegranate over a bowl to knock the seeds out.

Sprinkle the pistachios and pomegranate seeds over the tart.

Caramelized orange & mango custard tart

This recipe will teach you how to make the perfect smooth custard tart. There's a big fear of tackling these as they are notorious for leaking and over-baking into scrambled eggs. Don't feel under pressure to make your own pastry: 250g of ready-made pastry will do perfectly well. The most common mistake when making custard tarts is over-baking them, so check my tips on page 13 to learn when the wobble in the centre is just right. Also check out my tips on how to repair a pastry case (page 16) if you think you might have a potential leak before you pour the custard into it.

SERVES 8

Time required: 60 minutes preparation

Baking time: 30–35 minutes

Optimum oven position and setting: centre and fan

Essential equipment:
A 23cm non-stick tart tin with a loose bottom; mine is 35mm deep – the extra height is really useful for a slightly deeper tart
A baking sheet; mine is aluminium and measures 38 x 32cm
A temperature probe
A kitchen blowtorch

INGREDIENTS

1 quantity of sweet shortcrust pastry (page 15), blind baked in a 23cm tart tin (page 16)
6 medium eggs
finely grated zest of 2 oranges
140g caster sugar
90ml fresh smooth orange juice
50g mango purée (or use canned mangos, drained and puréed in a food processor)
1 tbsp spiced rum
135ml double cream
2 tbsp icing sugar

METHOD

Preheat the oven to 130°C fan/150°C/270°F/gas 2.

Crack the eggs into a large mixing bowl. Add the orange zest and caster sugar, and stir gently with a hand whisk until well combined. Add the orange juice, mango purée and the rum to the egg mixture, along with the cream. Stir gently until well mixed. Don't get too much air into the mixture.

Transfer the mixture to a saucepan and very gently heat to 50°C/120°F, stirring all the time. Alternatively, place the mixture in a heatproof jug and warm it in a microwave on low, stirring it every 30 seconds. Doing this gives the custard a head start on setting in the oven and means your pastry case won't over-bake.

Place the pastry case in its tin on a baking sheet and place on the oven shelf. Gently pour the custard filling into the pastry case until about 3mm from the top. Take care not to spill any on the outside of the pastry as that would make it stick to the tart tin.

Bake for 30–35 minutes until just set, with a wobble in the centre. You can test if the tart is baked to perfection by using a temperature probe: the centre should be just over 75°C/165°F.

Place on a wire rack and leave to cool completely before removing the tart from the tin. Once completely cooled, place in the fridge until required.

Just before serving, dust the icing sugar over the tart using a fine sieve and caramelize using a blowtorch.

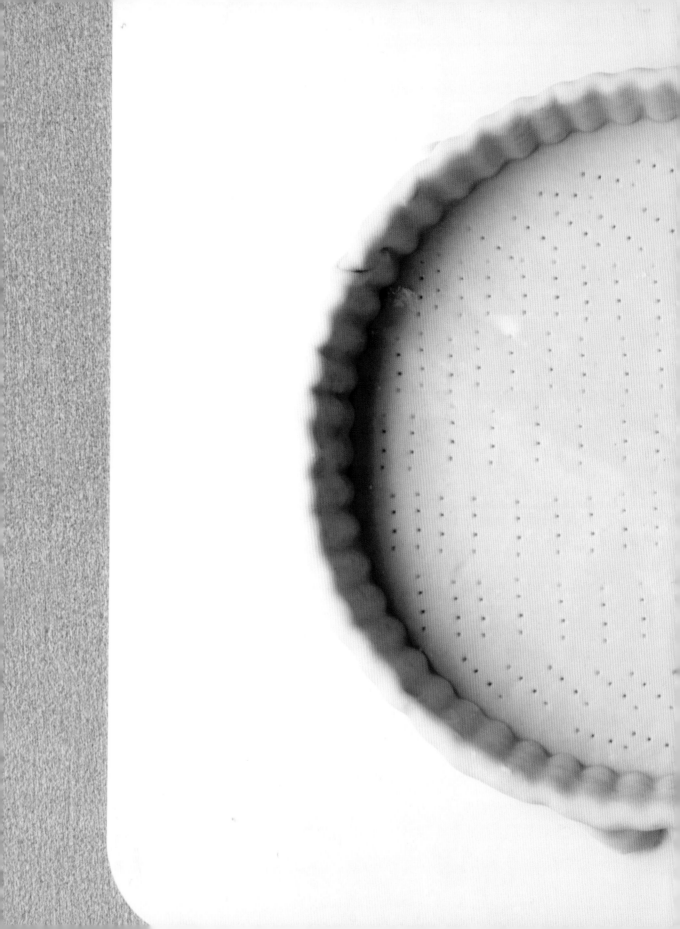

Sultana & Calvados custard tarts

The variety of small custard tarts baked around the world is simply mind-blowing. Some cultures use butter in the filling, others syrups, and I've even seen recipes using evaporated milk from the Far East. All I know is that a mini custard tart is one of life's great pleasures. I prefer them cold, but they can be enjoyed warm, too. My version has succulent sultanas hidden in the tangy Calvados-flavoured custard.

MAKES 12

Time required: 60 minutes preparation

Baking time: 25 minutes

Optimum oven position and setting: below centre and fan

Essential equipment:
A 12-hole non-stick muffin tin
An 11cm round fluted cutter
A temperature probe

INGREDIENTS

1 quantity of sweet shortcrust pastry (page 15)
4 medium egg yolks
45g caster sugar
340ml whole milk
½ tsp vanilla paste
2 tbsp Calvados
40g sultanas

METHOD

Divide the pastry in half. Roll out one half to a thickness of 3mm and then cut out six 11cm rounds. Place the rounds in the wells of the muffin tin. The top of the pastry should be just above the wells. Repeat with the remaining pastry. Place in the fridge for 30 minutes.

Preheat the oven to 180°C fan/200°C/360°F/gas 6.

Put the egg yolks into a large mixing bowl. Add the sugar and stir gently to dissolve; try not to get too much air into the mixture. Add the milk, vanilla and Calvados, and stir until well mixed and smooth.

Transfer the custard mixture to a saucepan and very gently heat it to 35°C/95°F, stirring all the time. Alternatively, place the mixture in a heatproof jug and warm it in a microwave on low, stirring it every 30 seconds. Transfer the mixture from the pan into a jug.

Take the muffin tin out of the fridge. Distribute the sultanas evenly among the pastry cases. Pour the custard mixture into the pastry cases, filling them three-quarters full. Don't be tempted to overfill them, as the mixture will expand and the pastry will shrink slightly.

Bake for 15 minutes, then reduce the temperature to 150°C fan/170°C /300°F/gas 3, and bake for a further 10 minutes.

The tarts are ready when the custard filling is just domed. You can test if they are baked to perfection by using a temperature probe: the centre of one should be just over 75°C/165°F. Leave the tarts to cool in the tin for 30 minutes. Remove and place on a wire rack to cool completely.

Keep in the fridge until required.

Butterscotch meringue tart

When I think butterscotch, I'm reminded of the dessert I was given at primary school. The unusual cream topping that graced the butterscotch had a strange shaving-foam texture. Thanks to that dessert, though, butterscotch is a firm flavour favorite among many adults today. So here's my modern twist on the dessert. A salted butterscotch filling in a crisp pastry case is topped with a flamed Italian meringue. I usually make it the day before I want it as the filling takes quite a while to set.

SERVES 8

Time required: 60 minutes preparation, plus at least 6 hours setting

Essential equipment:
A 23cm tart tin with a loose bottom; mine is 35mm deep – the extra height is really useful for a slightly deeper tart
A kitchen mixer fitted with a whisk
A sugar thermometer
A piping bag fitted with a 1cm plain round nozzle
A kitchen blowtorch

INGREDIENTS

1 quantity of sweet shortcrust pastry (page 15), blind baked in a 23cm tart tin (page 16)

For the butterscotch filling
3 tbsp plain flour
150ml whole milk
175g unsalted butter
360g soft brown sugar
¼ tsp sea salt flakes

For the Italian meringue topping
2 medium egg whites (80g)
¼ tsp cream of tartar
120g caster sugar
50ml water

METHOD

To make the filling, put the flour in a small bowl and add a little of the milk to make a smooth, runny paste.

Melt the butter in a saucepan over a medium heat. Add the remaining milk, sugar and salt, whisking all the time until the sugar has dissolved. Do not allow the mixture to boil. Whisk in the flour paste and keep stirring the mixture until it coats the back of a spoon.

Remove from the heat and allow to cool for 5 minutes before pouring the butterscotch into the pastry case. Leave to cool completely before placing in the fridge to set, preferably overnight.

Once the tart has set, remove it from the tin and place on your serving plate.

Make the Italian meringue. Place the egg whites in a spotlessly clean kitchen mixer bowl and whisk until soft peaks form. Add the cream of tartar and whisk again briefly.

Put the sugar and water in a saucepan and place over a medium heat; stir until the sugar dissolves. Increase the heat to high and bring the syrup to just over 115°C/240°F, using a sugar thermometer.

Start the mixer again at a medium speed and slowly trickle in the hot syrup. Increase the speed to full and whisk until the meringue becomes glossy, thick and cool.

Place the meringue in a piping bag fitted with a 1cm plain round nozzle and pipe the top of the tart with peaked columns of meringue. Keep in the fridge until required.

Toast the meringue with the blowtorch just before serving.

Chocolate simnel tart

The simnel cake is an Easter bake with origins that can be traced back over 700 years. It was usually eaten on the middle Sunday in Lent, when the forty-day fast was relaxed. Traditionally a fruit cake with two marzipan layers, one in the middle and one on top, it is decorated with 11 marzipan balls, to represent the Apostles.

Taking that as my inspiration, I came up with my simnel tart. The principles of the cake are all there, but I've added chocolate and topped it with cocoa-coated marzipan balls. A slice of this with a cup of tea is the perfect Easter afternoon treat.

SERVES 8

Time required: 60 minutes preparation

Baking time: 35 minutes

Optimum oven position and setting: below centre and fan

Essential equipment:
A 35 x 11cm rectangular tart tin with a loose bottom; mine is 25mm deep
A baking sheet; mine is aluminium and measures 38 x 32cm

INGREDIENTS

1 quantity of chocolate shortcrust pastry (page 15), blind baked in a 35 x 11cm rectangular tart tin (page 16)
3 tbsp cherry jam
50g dark chocolate (70% cocoa solids)
75g soft unsalted butter
75g caster sugar
1 large egg, beaten
40g self-raising flour
40g ground hazelnuts
25g dark chocolate chips
½ tsp ground cinnamon
⅛ tsp finely grated nutmeg
75g seedless raisins
25g dried morello cherries, finely chopped

To decorate
50g white chocolate
50ml double cream
140g white marzipan
25g unsweetened cocoa powder

METHOD

Preheat the oven to 170°C fan/190°C/340°F/gas 5.

Spread the cherry jam over the blind-baked pastry case.

Melt the chocolate in a heatproof bowl placed over a saucepan of simmering water. Make sure the water doesn't touch the bottom of the bowl. Alternatively, melt it in a microwave on low for a few minutes. Set aside.

Cream together the butter and sugar until pale and fluffy; this takes about 5 minutes in a kitchen mixer fitted with a paddle, or a little longer with a hand mixer. Beat in the egg and the flour. Now add the hazelnuts, chocolate chips, cinnamon, nutmeg, raisins and cherries, and fold until well combined. Finally, fold in the melted chocolate until well mixed. Spread this mixture evenly in the pastry case over the cherry jam.

Place the tart tin on a baking sheet and bake for about 35 minutes until the filling is risen and feels firm. A skewer inserted in the centre should come out clean.

Place on a wire rack and cool completely before removing the tart from the tin and placing it on your serving plate.

Melt the white chocolate and cream in a heatproof bowl placed over a saucepan of simmering water. Make sure the water doesn't touch the bottom of the bowl. Alternatively, melt in a microwave on low for a few minutes. Put the mixture into a disposable piping bag fitted with a 2mm plain round nozzle and drizzle over the top of the tart.

Divide the marzipan into 11 equal pieces and roll into balls. Roll the balls in the cocoa powder and place them in a row down the centre of the tart.

Pumpkin pie

The ultimate sweet baked pie from the United States, perfect for Halloween. Packed with spices with a deep, rich flavour, it goes perfectly with some vanilla ice cream on the side. For ease, I use a can of 100% natural ready-to-use pumpkin purée; this is available at most supermarkets, especially around Halloween.

If you are feeling playful, cut out a pumpkin face from a piece of cardboard (there is a template on page 252 for you to trace if you wish) and sprinkle desiccated coconut through it to decorate the tart.

This tart can be made the day before you need it and kept in the fridge overnight.

SERVES 10

Time required: 60 minutes preparation

Baking time: 50 minutes

Optimum oven position and setting: centre and fan

Essential equipment:
A 23cm tart tin with a loose bottom; mine is 35mm deep – the extra height is really useful for a slightly deeper tart
A baking sheet; mine is aluminium and measures 38 x 32cm

INGREDIENTS

1 quantity of sweet shortcrust pastry (page 15), blind baked in a 23cm tart tin (page 16)
2 large eggs
425g canned pumpkin purée
125g soft brown sugar
1 tsp ground cinnamon
1 tsp ground nutmeg
1 tsp ground ginger
1 tsp fine salt
410g evaporated milk

To decorate
30g desiccated coconut (optional)

METHOD

Preheat the oven to 200°C fan/220°C/390°F/gas 7.

Beat the eggs very lightly in a large bowl – you don't want to get any air into them. Stir in the pumpkin, sugar, spices, salt and evaporated milk, and place the filling in a large jug.

Place the blind-baked pastry case in its tin on a baking sheet and place on the oven shelf. Carefully pour the filling into the pastry case.

Bake for 15 minutes, and then reduce the oven temperature to 180°C fan/200°C/360°F/gas 6 and bake for a further 35 minutes. The filling should be almost set but still have a wobble in the centre. You can test if the tart is baked to perfection by using a temperature probe: the centre should be just over 75°C/165°F.

Place on a wire rack and leave to cool completely before removing from the tin. Place on your presentation plate. If you like, cut out a cardboard template in the shape of a pumpkin face, place on top of the tart and sprinkle desiccated coconut through the template.

Chocolate cherry tart with cherry brandy drizzles

A baked cherry chocolate tart set in a chocolate pastry case, this is a stunning showstopper, with syrup-filled pipettes thrown in for fun. It is decorated with kirsch-flavoured cream, chocolate ganache-filled cherries, chocolate cherry shapes and cherry brandy syrup drizzles. Don't be daunted by piping whipped cream: see my tip on page 63, and remember, practice makes perfect.

SERVES 12

Time required: 2 hours preparation

Baking time: 25–30 minutes

Optimum oven position and setting: centre and fan

Essential equipment:
A 26cm tart tin with a
    loose bottom; mine is
    30mm deep
Two baking sheets; mine are
    aluminium and measure
    38 x 32cm
A cherry stone pitter
Disposable piping bags,
    a wide star nozzle, a 5mm
    plain round nozzle and a
    3mm plain round nozzle
Small food decorating
    pipettes

INGREDIENTS
1 quantity of chocolate
    shortcrust pastry (page 15),
    blind baked in a 26cm tart
    tin (page 16)
375g dried morello cherries
3 tbsp cherry brandy
1 tsp kirsch
60ml boiling water

100g dark chocolate
    (70% cocoa solids)
125ml double cream
75ml whole milk
300g mascarpone cheese
3 medium eggs, beaten

Chocolate cherry shapes
30g dark chocolate
    (70% cocoa solids)

Cherries
40 fresh cherries
gold-coloured edible powder

Kirsch Chantilly cream
450ml double cream
3 tbsp icing sugar
1 tsp vanilla paste
5 tbsp kirsch

Chocolate ganache filling
50g dark chocolate
    (70% cocoa solids)
30ml double cream

Cherry brandy syrup
50ml cherry brandy
3 tsp icing sugar

METHOD
A few hours before you want to make the tart, or ideally the day before, place the dried morello cherries, cherry brandy, kirsch and boiling water in a heatproof bowl and stir well. Cover with clingfilm and set aside.

Preheat the oven to 180°C fan/200°C/360°F/gas 6.

Melt the chocolate, cream and milk in a heatproof bowl placed over a saucepan of simmering water, stirring occasionally until smooth and well blended. Make sure the water doesn't touch the bottom of the bowl. Set aside to cool for 5 minutes.

Stir in the mascarpone cheese, followed by the beaten eggs, until smooth and well blended – try not to get air in the mixture. Finally stir in the dried cherries along with any soaking liquid.

Place the pastry case in its tin on a baking sheet in the oven, then pour in the filling. Bake for 25–30 minutes until the filling feels firm in the centre and you start to see a little cracking around the edges. Place on a wire rack and leave to cool completely before removing the tart from the tin.

To make the chocolate cherry shapes, melt the chocolate in a heatproof bowl placed over a saucepan of simmering water. Make sure the water doesn't touch the bottom of the bowl. Alternatively, melt it in a microwave on low for a few minutes. Place in a small disposable piping bag and snip a small hole in it. Pipe six cherry shapes onto a piece of

continues overleaf...

non-stick baking parchment on a baking sheet and place in the fridge to set.

While the tart cools, remove the stones from the cherries, wipe dry with kitchen towel and brush them with the edible gold powder. Set aside.

To make the kirsch Chantilly cream, place all the ingredients in a bowl and whisk until just stiff. Divide the mixture equally between two piping bags, one fitted with a wide star nozzle and the other with a 5mm plain round nozzle.

To make the chocolate ganache, melt the chocolate with the cream in a heatproof bowl over a pan of simmering water until smooth and well blended. Place in the fridge to cool and firm up.

Put the cherry brandy in a small saucepan and warm over a low heat until hot but not boiling. Stir in the icing sugar and leave to cool.

To assemble: remove the tart from the tin and place on your presentation plate. Using the piping bag with the star nozzle, pipe Chantilly cream swirls around the edge of the tart. Make them large enough that each one can be topped with a cherry.

Using the piping bag with the plain nozzle, pipe small kisses of Chantilly cream about 2cm high to cover the exposed tart filling.

Place a cherry on each outer swirl with the hole facing up.

Take the chocolate ganache from the fridge and place in a small piping bag fitted with a 3mm plain round nozzle. Fill each of the remaining cherries. Place these filled cherries in an inner ring on top of the cream kisses.

Place the chocolate cherry shapes in a ring in the centre of the tart.

Count how many cherries you have on the outer circle and fill the same number of small food pipettes with cherry brandy syrup. Spear each cherry through the hole in the centre with a filled pipette.

Place in the fridge until required. Can be made the day before it's needed.

Variation
A SIMPLER VERSION
Make a simpler but still impressive version of this tart without the pipettes. Don't make the cherry brandy syrup or chocolate ganache filling. Keep the cherries whole and ideally with the stems still attached and brush them with the gold powder. Place them on top of the tart along with the chocolate cherry shapes.

Orange caramel mini tarts

I took my inspiration from the famous crème caramel when I came up with these tarts. Delve down through the orange liqueur-flavoured custard and you will find a slice of orange hidden in a semi-crunchy caramel layer. They are a great dinner party dessert and can be made well in advance and kept in the fridge. It's definitely worth sealing the base of the pastry for these. Serve with a little crème fraîche on the side.

SERVES 4

Time required:
60 minutes preparation

Baking time: 25–30 minutes

Optimum oven position and setting: centre and fan

Essential equipment:
Four 12cm loose-bottomed non-stick tart tins; mine are 30mm deep
A baking sheet; mine is aluminium and measures 38 x 32cm
A temperature probe
A strip zester

INGREDIENTS

1 quantity of sweet shortcrust pastry (page 15), blind baked in four 12cm tart tins and sealed with egg (see tip, page 16)
1 large orange, peeled and sliced into 3mm thick rounds

For the caramel
200g caster sugar
3 tbsp water

For the custard filling
6 medium eggs
140g caster sugar
90ml fresh smooth orange juice
2 tbsp orange liqueur
175ml double cream

To decorate
1 large orange, peeled and sliced into 3mm thick rounds
1 large orange, zested using a strip zester

METHOD

Preheat the oven to 130°C fan/150°C/270°F/gas 2. Place the pastry cases in their tins on a baking sheet. Put one slice of orange in the bottom of each pastry case.

To make the caramel, put the sugar and water in a saucepan over a medium heat until the sugar starts to dissolve and turn golden. Do not stir until it's virtually all dissolved. Once the caramel is smooth and golden, dip the bottom of the pan into some cold water to stop it cooking. Let it cool for a minute, then pour a little into each tart tin, covering the orange slices completely. Place on one side to set.

To make the custard filling, crack the eggs into a large mixing bowl. Add the sugar and stir gently with a hand whisk until well combined. Add the orange juice, liqueur and cream, and stir gently until well mixed. Don't get too much air into the mixture.

Transfer the mixture to a saucepan and gently heat to 50°C/120°F, stirring all the time. Alternatively, place the mixture in a heatproof jug and warm in a microwave on low, stirring every 30 seconds. This gives the custard a head start on setting, so your pastry case won't over-bake.

Place the tart cases on the baking sheet into the oven and gently pour the custard filling into each tart case until about 3mm from the top. Take care not to spill any on the outside of the pastry as that would make it stick to the tart tins.

Bake for 25–30 minutes until just set with a wobble in the centre. You can test if the tarts are baked to perfection by using a temperature probe: the centre should be just over 75°C/165°F.

Place the tarts on a wire rack and leave to cool completely before removing from the tins. Once cooled, decorate the top with orange slices and some thin strands of zest, then place in the fridge until required.

Asparagus & pancetta tart

This is a luxurious tart that uses asparagus and crispy fried pancetta, but we all deserve a treat every now and then. It looks fabulous too. Served with a light salad it makes the perfect summer lunch or supper. It keeps well in the fridge, so make it the day before and package it up for a picnic delight.

I use small, tender asparagus tips for this tart. Don't be tempted to add any salt to the recipe as the pancetta and Parmesan cheese will complete the seasoning for you.

SERVES 8

Time required:
75 minutes preparation

Baking time: 30 minutes

Optimum oven position and setting: below centre and fan

Essential equipment:
You will need a 35 x 11cm rectangular tart tin with a loose bottom, mine is 2.5cm deep
A baking sheet; mine is aluminium and measures 38 x 32cm

INGREDIENTS

1 quantity of shortcrust pastry (page 15), blind baked in a 35 x 11cm rectangular tart tin (page 16)
40 asparagus tips
250g smoked pancetta, cut into 1cm cubes
2 medium eggs
225ml double cream
freshly ground black pepper
25g Parmesan cheese, finely grated

METHOD

Preheat the oven to 160°C fan/180°C/320°F/gas 4.

Cook the asparagus in a large pan of boiling water over a medium heat for 3–4 minutes until just tender. Drain and place in a bowl of ice-cold water for 5 minutes to stop them cooking.

Dry fry the pancetta in a frying pan over a medium heat until just crisp. Drain on kitchen paper.

Dry the asparagus and trim them to the width of the tin. Cut the trimmings into 1cm pieces. Mix the asparagus trimmings and pancetta together and spread them over the pastry case. Place the tart tin on a baking sheet.

Crack the eggs into a jug and gently whisk in the cream and a few twists of black pepper. Add the Parmesan and whisk again. Pour about two-thirds of the egg mixture over the pancetta in the tart case.

Lay the asparagus tips along the length of the tart. Gently spoon the remaining egg mixture over the asparagus. Take care not to overfill the pastry case.

Carefully place the tart in the oven and bake for 30 minutes. You can test if the tart is baked to perfection by using a temperature probe: the centre should be just over 75°C/165°F.

Place on a wire rack and leave to cool in the tin for 30 minutes before placing on your presentation plate. Eat warm or cold.

Tortilla tart

To me, the Spanish tortilla is the ultimate comfort food. I was brought up on them. In the winter served hot, amazing. Cold from the fridge in the summer, fantastic. I can virtually make one with my eyes closed after watching my mum make them hundreds of times. I'll even pop a slice between two slices of white bread sometimes... wrong, but oh so right! So what better than to put the tortilla in a pastry case? It's like all my Christmases have come at once. Cold, this is a brilliant tart and perfect for a picnic, packed lunch, or cheeky late-night snack.

SERVES 8

Time required: 90 minutes preparation

Cooking time:
30–35 minutes for the potatoes, 30 minutes baking

Optimum oven position and setting: below centre and fan

Essential equipment:
A 23cm tart tin with a loose bottom; mine is 35mm deep – the extra height is really useful for a slightly deeper tart
A large non-stick frying pan with a lid
A baking sheet; mine is aluminium and measures 38 x 32cm

INGREDIENTS

1 quantity of shortcrust pastry (page 15), blind baked in a 23cm tart tin (page 16)
1 tbsp olive oil (not extra virgin)
1 medium onion, finely sliced
750g (after peeling) charlotte potatoes, sliced into 3mm rounds
½ tsp fine salt
½ tsp freshly ground black pepper
1 tbsp water
125g frozen peas, blanched in boiling water and drained
4 medium eggs, beaten
70ml whole milk

METHOD

Preheat the oven to 160°C fan/180°C/320°F/gas 4.

Put the olive oil, onion, potatoes, salt, pepper and water in a large frying pan and stir to coat everything in the oil. Place a lid on the pan and cook gently over a low heat for 30–35 minutes. Turn the potatoes over gently every 10 minutes. When they are tender, take the pan off the heat and leave to cool for 10 minutes.

Place the tart tin on a baking sheet and place a thin layer of the potatoes and onions in the pastry case. Sprinkle the peas evenly over the mixture. Put another layer of the potato and onion mixture on top to fill the tart, using some perfect potatoes for the top layer.

Put the eggs and milk in a mixing bowl or jug and beat together until well combined. Slowly pour the egg mixture over the potatoes, letting it fill in all the gaps.

Give the tart a grind of black pepper and bake for 30 minutes. You can test if it is baked to perfection by using a temperature probe: the centre should be just over 75°C/165°F. The potatoes should feel soft if a skewer is pushed into the centre.

Place on a wire rack and leave to cool completely before removing the tart from the tin.

Cheese & onion flan

Here we have my mother-in-law Rita's legendary cheese and onion flan. She has been baking this for as long as I can remember. You can guarantee it will always make an appearance at a family buffet, causing a stampede. In fact, it's so popular she always makes two now! It's a fantastic bake warm or cold, at any time of day. A slice with a side salad makes a perfect supper.

METHOD

Preheat the oven to 180°C fan/200°C/360°F/gas 6.

Put the butter and onions in a large frying pan over a low heat and fry gently until cooked through and translucent. Drain on kitchen paper.

Put the eggs and milk in a large mixing bowl and stir until well combined. Stir in the salt, pepper, cayenne and finally the cheese.

Place the tart tin on a baking sheet and spread the onions evenly in the pastry case. Carefully pour in the cheese mixture and level it out with a spatula.

Bake for 25–30 minutes. You can test if the flan is baked to perfection by using a temperature probe: the centre should be just over 75°C/165°F.

Place on a wire rack and leave to cool completely before removing the tart from the tin.

SERVES 14

Time required: 60 minutes preparation

Baking time: 25–30 minutes

Optimum oven position and setting: below centre and fan

Essential equipment:
A 26cm tart tin with a loose bottom; mine is 30mm deep
A baking sheet; mine is aluminium and measures 38 x 32cm

INGREDIENTS

1 quantity of shortcrust pastry (page 15), blind baked in a 26cm tart tin (page 16)
25g unsalted butter
3 red onions, finely sliced – you need about 350g
5 medium eggs, beaten
75ml whole milk
¼ tsp fine salt
½ tsp freshly ground black pepper
¼ tsp cayenne pepper
175g mature Cheddar cheese, coarsely grated

CHAPTER 6
Pies & pastries

LEAFY
PASTRY TOP

1. **Mum's apple pie**
A shortcrust pastry pie cooked in a round pie dish with spiced apples and a spectacular top of pastry made from cut-out leaf shapes.

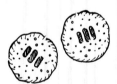

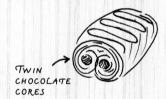

TWIN
CHOCOLATE
CORES

2. **Hot water crust pork pies**
   – Pork & chorizo pie
   – Pork, asparagus & sun-dried tomato picnic piep
   – Pork, chicken & cranberry pie

3. **Prune & apricot brandy cakes**
My take on the popular Manchester Eccles cake made with a cheat's puff pastry.

4. **Chocolate orange mince pie turnovers**
My take on the traditional mince pie.

5. **Galette des rois**
The traditional Epiphany puff pastry cake with a hidden charm. Mine is frangipane and plum-flavoured.

6. **Danish pastries**
How to make Danish yeasted laminated pastry easily and quickly. Then recipes for the following:
– Chocolate & salted caramel swirls
– Pains au chocolat
– Nut & raisin vanilla turnovers

7. **Choux pastry**
How to make sweet and chocolate choux pastries easily without failure. Then recipes for the following to teach different piping and baking techniques:

8. **Eclairs**
– Strawberry cheesecake éclairs with a strawberry jam and cream cheese filling
– Chocca mocca éclairs with candied walnuts
– Lemon meringue éclairs with flamed Italian meringue topping

NIBBED SUGAR

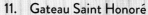

9. **Chouquettes**
Bite-size light balls of choux with a crackle top. Two flavour variations – matcha green tea and chocolate hazelnut.

10. **Chocolate heaven profiteroles**
Chocolate smothered and filled profiteroles. Great dessert dish.

11. **Gateau Saint Honoré**
A puff-pastry base with choux ring and cream-filled choux balls coated in caramel. Topped with summer fruits and pecan nuts coated in caramel. A great showstopper.

Mum's apple pie

This was a Sunday dinner staple in my house when I was growing up. Apple pie drowned in custard is just the best. The pastry was thin and crisp, the apples succulently soft inside. I have updated it with a fabulous lid made from cut-out pastry leaves; it's a labour of love, but well worth the effort. You can make it several hours in advance and keep it in the fridge until you want to bake it. If you don't have time to make the leaves, just roll a second disc of pastry to use as a lid and pierce a couple of holes in it to let the steam out.

SERVES 8

Time required: 60 minutes preparation, plus chilling

Baking time: about 60 minutes

Optimum oven position and setting: below centre and fan

Essential equipment:
A 24cm diameter shallow pie plate with a wide rim; I use an enamelled metal plate
A leaf cutter will speed things up a little; the cutter I use is 4.5 x 2.5cm

INGREDIENTS

1 quantity of shortcrust pastry (page 15)
4 Braeburn or Granny Smith apples, peeled, cored and cut into 5mm wedges
finely grated zest of 1 unwaxed lemon
1 tbsp lemon juice
75g golden caster sugar
2 tbsp plain flour, plus extra for dusting
1 tsp ground cinnamon
¼ tsp ginger
pinch of fine salt
30g soft unsalted butter, plus extra for greasing

METHOD

Grease the pie plate with butter and dust with flour.

Cut the pastry in half. On a well-floured surface, roll out one half to a circle larger than the pie plate, 3mm thick. Place the pastry on the pie plate and trim off the excess. Place in the fridge while you make the filling.

Prepare the apples and place them in a bowl with the lemon zest and juice. Toss thoroughly; the acid in the lemon will stop the apples browning too much.

In a separate bowl, mix the sugar, flour, cinnamon, ginger and salt. Toss the apples in the mixture to coat them all well.

Take the pie plate out of the fridge and layer the apples in the pastry, forming a dome shape. Don't place any apples on the pastry rim. Dot the apples with the butter. Place back in the fridge.

Roll out the remaining pastry on a well-floured surface and cut out as many leaves as you can.

Take the pie plate out of the fridge and brush a little water around the rim. Start placing leaves around the rim, overlapping them slightly and brushing the bottom of each leaf with a little water. Continue to place leaves on the pie in concentric circles until the apples are completely covered. You don't have to press the leaves down. Place the pie back in the fridge for 30 minutes.

While the pie is chilling, preheat the oven to 190°C fan/210°C/375°F/gas 6½.

Bake for 10 minutes, then turn the oven temperature down to 170°C fan/190°C/340°F/gas 5 and bake for a further 45–50 minutes until golden.

Place on a wire rack to cool. Serve warm or cold, directly from the pie plate.

Hot water crust pork pies

Being a Northerner, I'm passionate about pies. I have a particular need for pork pies on a regular basis. I can't resist hot water crust pastry, it's such a brilliant pie casing and delicious too. So here are three recipes for hot water crust pork pies. I usually make them the day before I want them. In my opinion, they are much better the next day after resting in the fridge overnight.

Some words of advice when making hot water crust pies. If you are using a round tin, always use a non-stick springform one. Inevitably pork pies do leak a little out of the vent holes when baking, and it tends to dribble down the sides and get sticky (using fresh rather than frozen meat will reduce the amount of liquid). A greased springform tin makes life much easier when you want to release the pie.

Get creative too. The lid of a pie is just begging to be decorated. I use fondant cutters to make decorations that look amazing. Letter-shaped cutters are brilliant for personalizing a pie.

Finally, and this is really important, when using raw meats in a pie always check the internal temperature to make sure it is baked correctly (see page 13). If the centre hasn't reached the right temperature, it's not ready.

Pork & chorizo pie

I make this pie in a rectangular loaf tin. Great for dinner served with a fresh salad or perfect for a picnic, this pie has some great Spanish flavours. It looks spectacular: not only can you let your creativity go wild when decorating the top, every slice reveals a perfect round of chorizo surrounded in seasoned pork.

METHOD

Preheat the oven to 200°C fan/220°C/390°F/gas 7.

Place the minced pork in a large bowl. Add the onion, garlic, chilli, paprika, pepper, salt and breadcrumbs. Mix until well combined.

Make the hot water crust pastry and roll out two-thirds of it to a thickness of about 4mm. You shouldn't need to flour your surface when rolling out as this pastry is self-greasing. If it does break or split in places, you can just patch it up. Line the tin with the pastry, leaving an overhang all the way round.

Put a 1.5cm thick layer of the pork mixture in the base of the tin and then place a strip of the chorizos down the middle. I cut the ends off the chorizos for neatness, so you get a perfect cylinder all the way through.

Place the rest of the pork around and on top of the chorizo. It should be enough to fill the rest of the tin. Compact it well.

Roll out the remaining pastry about 4mm thick into a rectangle larger than the tin to make the lid.

Using a pastry brush, brush egg yolk all around the rim of the pie and place the lid on it. Press down firmly to make a good seal and then trim off the excess. Using your fingers, neatly crimp all around the edge. I use a 1cm round piping nozzle to cut out two holes in the top of the pie so the steam can escape.

Re-roll the pastry trimmings to 3mm thick. I use a pastry cutter to make some pretty leaf shapes, but you can make any shapes you like.

Brush all over the top of the pie with egg yolk and place your cut-out decorations on top. Then give those a brushing of yolk too.

Now here's the key to success with a hot water crust pastry pie to prevent sogginess. Place the pie on a baking sheet to catch any excess liquid that may come out during baking and put in the hot oven just below the centre. Bake for 30 minutes. Don't open the oven door during this period as we want the outside of the pie to crisp up.

Loosely place a piece of foil on the pie to prevent the top burning and reduce the oven temperature to 180°C fan/200°C/350°F/gas 6. Bake for a further 60–80 minutes. If you are getting excess liquid spilling out of the pie and onto the lid, use a piece of kitchen towel to mop it up every now and then while baking.

After 60 minutes, check the internal temperature of the pie. It should be 75°C/167°F. If it hasn't reached that temperature, it isn't ready. Check again at 10-minute intervals.

Leave the pie to cool in the tin for 15 minutes before releasing it and placing on a wire rack to cool completely.

Once totally cool, keep in the fridge.

SERVES 12

Time required: 60 minutes preparation

Baking time: 1½ –2 hours

Optimum oven position and setting: below centre and fan

Essential equipment:
A 900g/2lb loaf tin; the base of mine measures 95 x 195mm and the tin is 70mm high. Grease it with a thin coating of lard
A baking sheet; mine is aluminium and measures 38 x 32cm

INGREDIENTS

1 quantity of hot water crust pastry (page 19)
750g minced pork
1 small white onion, finely chopped
1 garlic clove, finely chopped
½ tsp chilli flakes
1 tsp sweet (*dulce*) smoked paprika
½ tsp freshly ground black pepper
½ tsp fine salt
25g natural breadcrumbs
200g whole mini raw chorizo sausages (available from most supermarkets)
2 medium egg yolks, beaten, for gluing and glazing

Pork, asparagus & sun-dried tomato picnic pie

Taking a slice of this pie reveals a layer of asparagus topped with sun-dried tomatoes, sandwiched by fragrant pork and dry-cured bacon. Make it the day before you want it. It really improves after having been kept in the fridge overnight.

SERVES 12

Time required: 60 minutes preparation

Optimum oven position and setting: below centre and fan

Essential equipment:
A 20cm non-stick springform cake tin. Grease it with a thin coating of lard or butter
A baking sheet; mine is aluminium and measures 38 x 32cm

INGREDIENTS

1 quantity of hot water crust pastry (page 19)
700g minced pork
1 tsp fresh thyme, finely chopped
3 tbsp fresh parsley, finely chopped
1 tsp freshly ground black pepper
1 tsp fine salt
finely grated zest of 1 unwaxed lemon
25g natural breadcrumbs
200g dry-cured bacon, coarsely chopped
250g asparagus tips, trimmed and cut in half
100g sun-dried tomatoes, drained and cut into thin slices

METHOD

Preheat the oven to 200°C fan/220°C/390°F/gas 7.

Place the minced pork in a large bowl and add the thyme, parsley, pepper, salt, lemon zest and breadcrumbs. Mix until well combined. Add the bacon and mix again.

Make the hot water crust pastry and roll out two-thirds of it to a thickness of about 4mm. You shouldn't need to flour your surface when rolling out as this pastry is self-greasing. If it does break or split in places, you can just patch it up. Line the tin with the pastry, leaving an overhang all the way round.

Put half of the pork in an even layer in the base of the tin. Place the asparagus tips on the pork, radiating from the centre. Evenly distribute the sun-dried tomatoes on top of the asparagus. Add the rest of the pork and flatten the top.

Roll out the remaining pastry about 4mm thick into a disc larger than the tin to make the lid.

Using a pastry brush, brush egg yolk all around the rim of the pie and place the lid on it. Press down firmly to make a good seal and then trim off the excess. Using your fingers, neatly crimp all around the edge. I use a 1cm round piping nozzle to cut out three holes in the top of the pie so the steam can escape.

Re-roll the pastry trimmings to 3mm thick. I use a fondant cutter to make a flowers and stars landscape, but you can cut any shapes you like.

Brush all over the top of the pie with egg yolk and place your cut-out decorations on top. Then give those a brushing of yolk too.

Now here's the key to success with a hot water crust pastry pie to prevent sogginess. Place the pie on a baking sheet to catch any excess liquid that may come out during baking and put in the hot oven just below the centre. Bake for 30 minutes. Don't open the oven door during this period as we want the outside of the pie to crisp up.

Loosely place a piece of foil on the pie to prevent the top burning and reduce the oven temperature to 180°C fan/200°C/350°F/gas 6. Bake for a further 60–80 minutes. If you are getting excess liquid spilling out of the pie and onto the lid, use a piece of kitchen towel to mop it up every now and then while baking.

After 60 minutes, check the internal temperature of the pie. It should be 75°C/167°F. If it hasn't reached that temperature, it isn't ready. Check again at 10-minute intervals.

Leave the pie to cool in the tin for 15 minutes before releasing it and placing on a wire rack to cool completely. Once totally cool, keep in the fridge.

Pork, chicken & cranberry pie

This is a fabulous pie to make during Christmas, but don't just save it just for then – it's great at any time of the year. Two layers of spiced pork sandwich a succulent layer of chicken breast which is topped with dried cranberries and redcurrant jelly. Check out my tip on how to fill a pie with jelly.

SERVES 12

Time required: 60 minutes preparation

Baking time: 1½ –2 hours

Optimum oven position and setting: below centre and fan

Essential equipment:
A 20cm non-stick springform cake tin. Grease it with a thin coating of lard or butter
A baking sheet; mine is aluminium and measures 38 x 32cm

INGREDIENTS

1 quantity of hot water crust pastry (page 19)
600g minced pork
1 tsp ground mace
1 tsp ground black pepper
¼ tsp cayenne pepper
1 tbsp fresh sage, finely chopped
1 garlic clove, finely chopped
1 tsp fine salt
25g natural breadcrumbs
100g dried cranberries
3 tbsp redcurrant jelly
400g chicken breasts, skinned and cubed
2 medium egg yolks, beaten, for gluing and glazing

METHOD

Preheat the oven to 200°C fan/220°C/390°F/gas 7.

Place the minced pork in a large bowl and add the mace, black pepper, cayenne, sage, garlic, salt and breadcrumbs. Mix until well combined.

Place the cranberries and redcurrant jelly in a small bowl and mix well.

Make the hot water crust pastry and roll out two-thirds of it to a thickness of about 4mm. You shouldn't need to flour your surface when rolling out as this pastry is self-greasing. If it does break or split in places, you can just patch it up. Line the tin with the pastry, leaving an overhang all the way round.

Put half of the pork in an even layer in the base of the tin. Place the chicken on the pork in an even layer. Spread the cranberry mixture evenly on top of the chicken. Add the rest of the pork and flatten the top.

Roll out the remaining pastry about 4mm thick into a disc larger than the tin to make the lid.

Using a pastry brush, brush egg yolk all around the rim of the pie and place the lid on it. Press down firmly to make a good seal and then trim off the excess. Using your fingers, neatly crimp all around the edge. I use a 1cm round piping nozzle to cut out three holes in the top of the pie so the steam can escape.

Re-roll the pastry trimmings to 3mm thick. I use a fondant cutter to make decorations. If it's Christmas, make some holly leaves or snowflakes.

Brush all over the top of the pie with egg yolk and place your cut-out decorations on top. Then give those a brushing of yolk too.

Now here's the key to success with a hot water crust pastry pie to prevent sogginess. Place the pie on a baking sheet to catch any excess liquid that may come out during baking and put in the hot oven just below the centre. Bake for 30 minutes. Don't open the oven door during this period as we want the outside of the pie to crisp up.

Loosely place a piece of foil on the pie to prevent the top burning and reduce the oven temperature to 180°C fan/ 200°C/350°F/gas 6. Bake for a further 60–80 minutes.

If you are getting excess liquid spilling out of the pie and onto the lid, use a piece of kitchen towel to mop it up every now and then while baking.

After 60 minutes, check the internal temperature of the pie. It should be 75°C/167°F. If it hasn't reached that temperature, it isn't ready. Check again at 10-minute intervals.

Leave the pie to cool in the tin for 15 minutes before releasing it and placing on a wire rack to cool completely.

Once totally cool, keep in the fridge.

TIP

Filling a pie with jelly

Any pie can be filled with jelly while it is still warm just after baking. The jelly is made from stock and gelatine. For a 20cm pie, you will need about 600ml of chicken stock. I use gelatine leaves, and four leaves will set 470ml of liquid, but check the instructions for making a firm set jelly on your packet of gelatine. Place the leaves in cold water for a couple of minutes and place the stock in a small saucepan to warm up; don't boil it. Squeeze the excess water from the gelatine and add it to the warm stock; stir until dissolved. Place the stock in a jug and, using a small funnel, very slowly pour the stock into the cooled pie through one of the vent holes in the top. It might take a few minutes for the stock to work its way around inside. Stop when you see the stock in the holes. Let the pie stand at room temperature for an hour before placing in the fridge overnight.

Prune & apricot brandy cakes

Eccles cakes are a staple in my, and probably many other Mancunian's, diet. They are named after the town of Eccles, but I read recently they don't have protected geographical status, so they can be made in any part of the country, which is just wrong in my opinion. Really flaky buttery pastry holds a filling of delicious raisins and currants. Affectionately known as a squashed fly cake, it always makes me chuckle when I tuck into one. Since they were my inspiration, I dedicate my prune and apricot brandy cakes to the famous Eccles cake.

MAKES 10 CAKES

Time required: 60 minutes preparation

Baking time: 15–20 minutes

Optimum oven position and setting: centre and fan

Essential equipment:
Two baking sheets; mine are aluminium and measure 38 x 32cm. Line with non-stick baking parchment
An 11cm round cutter

INGREDIENTS

1 quantity of cheat's puff pastry (page 20)
125g prunes, finely chopped
75g dried apricots, finely chopped
⅛ tsp grated nutmeg
2 tbsp brandy
finely grated zest of 1 unwaxed lemon
100g light brown sugar
25g unsalted butter
1 medium egg white, beaten
1 tbsp demerara sugar

METHOD

The night before you want to make the cakes, place the prunes, apricots, spices and brandy in a bowl. Stir well, cover and leave overnight.

Preheat the oven to 200°C fan/220°C/390°F/gas 7.

Add the lemon zest and sugar to the fruits and stir well. Melt the butter in a small saucepan and stir into the fruit mixture.

Cut the pastry in half. On a floured surface, roll out one half to about 3mm thick and cut out five 11cm rounds. Place a tablespoon of the fruit mixture in the centre of each round, brush the edges with water and then gather the pastry around the filling and squeeze it firmly to seal. Turn the cakes over, dust your hands with a little flour and flatten each cake slightly.

Place all five cakes on a baking sheet, evenly spaced apart, and brush with the beaten egg white. Sprinkle with a little demerara sugar and cut three 1cm slits in the top of each cake.

Bake for 15–20 minutes until golden. Place on a wire rack to cool.

Make the second batch while the first batch is baking.

Chocolate orange mince pie turnovers

Early mince pies had meats such as mutton in them; they are thought to originate in the Middle East, and you can see traces of the iconic British bake in Middle Eastern cookery today, with the use of spices and fruits in savoury dishes. Don't worry, though, I've stayed clear of mutton in my version. I've used shop-bought puff pastry and added some chocolate chips and orange zest to good-quality mincemeat. Trust me, if you've never had chocolate chips in mincemeat before you are in for a treat.

MAKES 12

Time required: 40 minutes preparation

Baking time: 15–20 minutes

Optimum oven position and setting: centre and fan

Essential equipment: Two baking sheets; mine are aluminium and measure 38 x 32cm. Line with non-stick baking parchment

INGREDIENTS
150g mincemeat
50g dark chocolate chips
finely grated zest of 1 orange
500g ready-made puff pastry
15g flaked almonds
1 medium egg, beaten
25g caster sugar

METHOD
Preheat the oven to 200°C fan/220°C/390°F/gas 7.

Put the mincemeat, chocolate chips and orange zest in a bowl and mix well.

Cut the pastry in half. Roll out one half on a lightly floured surface to a rectangle and trim it neatly to 36 x 24cm. Cut the rectangle into six 12cm squares.

Place a heaped teaspoon of the mincemeat in the centre of each square. Sprinkle a few almonds on top of the filling. Brush the edges neatly with a little beaten egg and fold the pastry over diagonally to make a triangular parcel. Seal the parcel edges firmly with the back of a fork and place on a prepared baking sheet. Place in the fridge when you have made six.

Repeat with the remaining pastry on a separate baking sheet and place in the fridge.

Take the first six out of the fridge and brush the tops with egg. Using a sharp knife, gently score a design into the top of each parcel, being careful not to go through the pastry. Then make two small slits in the top of each parcel. Sprinkle a little sugar on each one and bake for 15–20 minutes until golden and risen.

Bake the second tray of turnovers. Can be eaten warm or cold.

Galette des rois

The *galette des rois*, or kings' cake, is traditionally eaten in France to celebrate the Christian feast of Epiphany on 6 January, also known as Twelfth Night. My version is a puff pastry cake filled with an almond and hazelnut frangipane, complemented with prunes and plum jam.

A trinket known as a *fève* is usually hidden in the cake. Whoever finds the figurine is crowned 'king' or 'queen' of the celebration. If you don't have a figurine, use a dried bean instead (*fève* actually means 'bean'). A gold paper crown is sometimes placed on the cake just before serving, ready for presentation to the king or queen.

METHOD

Preheat the oven to 200°C fan/220°C/390°F/gas 7.

Cut the pastry block in half. Roll out one half on a lightly floured surface and cut out a circle 26cm in diameter. Roll out the other half and cut out a circle 28cm in diameter. Place the two circles on the baking sheets and place in the fridge to chill while you make the filling.

Cream together the butter and icing sugar in a bowl, using a whisk, until just fluffy. Add the eggs, almonds, hazelnuts, flour, brandy and vanilla paste, and fold in until well combined and smooth.

Take the smaller circle of pastry and spread the jam over it, leaving an uncoated border of about 3cm around the edge.

Place the frangipane mix in a disposable piping bag and cut off the end, making a hole about 1.5cm in diameter. Pipe the frangipane over the jam to a thickness of about 1.5cm. You may have a little left over; do not overfill the cake.

Lay the prune slices evenly over the frangipane. If you are placing a trinket in the cake, place it in the frangipane now.

Brush a little water on the exposed pastry around the edge and gently place the larger circle of pastry on top; press the edges firmly to seal. Brush the top with egg but be careful not to get any egg on the edges or the pastry will not rise. Using a sharp knife, gently score a design into the top of the cake, being careful not to go through the pastry. Lastly, make two small holes in the centre of the cake to allow steam to escape.

Bake for about 30 minutes, until golden and risen. Can be eaten warm or cold. Best eaten on the day of baking.

SERVES 8

Time required: 30 minutes preparation

Baking time: 30 minutes

Optimum oven position and setting: centre and fan

Essential equipment:
Two baking sheets; mine are aluminium and measure 38 x 32cm. Line with non-stick baking parchment
Two discs (26cm and 28cm) to use as templates to cut out the pastry rounds; I use a couple of tart tin loose bottoms

INGREDIENTS

500g ready-made puff pastry
125g unsalted butter, at room temperature
125g icing sugar
2 medium eggs
85g ground almonds
40g ground hazelnuts
2 tbsp plain flour, plus extra for rolling out
1 tsp brandy (optional)
½ tsp vanilla paste (or 1 tsp vanilla extract)
4 tbsp plum jam
85g moist, ready-to-eat prunes, thinly sliced
1 medium egg, beaten, for glazing

Danish pastries

There's something really satisfying about making Danish pastries. Those crumbly flakes of pastry that just melt in the mouth are to die for. The variations and fillings you can use are pretty much endless and hopefully my recipes will set you off down a road to experiment and try your own.

My recipes will show you three different ways of shaping the pastries as well as completely different fillings and toppings. Feel free to try ready-made custards, spreads and canned fruits when making your own. I usually make the pastry a day or two before I need it and keep it wrapped in the fridge.

Danish pastry dough

METHOD

Put the milk in a heatproof jug and add the boiling water to give you a warm liquid.

Place all the remaining ingredients except the butter in a large mixing bowl. When adding the yeast and salt, place them at opposite sides of the bowl. Add two-thirds of the liquid and begin to mix it all together with your fingers – or use a kitchen mixer with a dough hook. Add more liquid gradually until all the dry ingredients are picked up and you have a soft dough. You may not need all of the liquid.

Tip the mixture out onto a clean surface and knead it for about 10 minutes. You will work through the initial wet stage and eventually end up with a smooth, soft, silky dough. If you are using a kitchen mixer, knead it for about 6 minutes.

Lightly oil a large bowl and place the dough in it. Cover it with clingfilm or a shower cap and place it in the fridge for 2 hours to prove.

While the dough is proving, place the cold butter between two pieces of non-stick baking parchment and flatten it out to a 33 x 19cm rectangle, using a rolling pin. Place it on a baking sheet and pop it in the fridge to harden again.

When the dough has proved, tip it out onto a floured surface and roll it out to a 50 x 20cm rectangle.

With a short edge nearest to you, place the flattened butter on the lower two-thirds of the dough. Fold the top third of dough over and then fold the bottom third upwards so all the butter is encased. Press the edges firmly to seal it in.

Turn the block of dough 90 degrees and roll it out again to a rectangle 50 x 20cm – use the rolling pin in a pressing action at first to make ridges and evenly distribute the butter inside. Fold the top third down and the bottom third up, wrap in clingfilm and place in the fridge for 20 minutes to let the butter harden up again.

Repeat the rolling and folding process twice more, placing it in the fridge between folds.

After the last roll and fold let the dough chill in the fridge for an hour or overnight.

MAKES 12 PAINS AU CHOCOLAT, OR 18 TURNOVERS, OR 18 SWIRLS

Time required: 60 minutes preparation and one prove

Essential equipment:
A rolling pin and non-stick baking parchment for flattening the butter

INGREDIENTS

125ml whole milk
75ml boiling water
500g strong white bread flour
10g instant yeast
75g golden caster sugar
2 medium eggs, beaten
1 tsp fine salt
250g cold unsalted butter

Chocolate & salted caramel swirls

Here is a classic swirl Danish with a twist, literally! These are popular in a cinnamon variation, but with a chocolate and salted caramel drizzle they are just to die for. It's best to make both the dough and the chocolate crème pâtissière the day before and keep them in the fridge overnight. Feel free to use shop-bought custard if you don't have time to make the crème pâtissière. They won't be as chocolatey but will still be delicious.

MAKES 18 PASTRIES

Time required: 45 minutes preparation and one prove

Baking time: 20–25 minutes

Optimum oven position and setting: centre and no fan, with a baking stone

Essential equipment:
Two baking sheets; mine are aluminium and measure 38 x 32cm. Line with non-stick baking parchment
A couple of large bags to put the baking sheets into for proving

INGREDIENTS

1 quantity of Danish pastry dough (page 175)
1 quantity (approx. 500g) of chocolate crème pâtissière (page 22), cold
100g milk chocolate chips
1 medium egg, beaten, for glazing

For the salted caramel sauce
100g caster sugar
1 tbsp water
75ml double cream
50g soft unsalted butter
½ tsp fine salt
½ tsp coarse sea salt flakes

METHOD

On a well-floured surface, roll out the block of Danish pastry to a 36 x 30cm rectangle.

With the long edge nearest you, spread the crème pâtissière evenly over the dough. Sprinkle the chocolate chips evenly over the crème pâtissière.

Roll the rectangle up tightly like a Swiss roll, starting at one long edge.

Using a sharp knife, cut the roll into 18 equal pieces; each piece should be about 2cm thick.

Place nine pieces on a lined baking sheet, flattening them down slightly. Place the baking sheet in a large bag and prove for 45 minutes at room temperature. Make sure the bag doesn't touch the dough.

Repeat for the second nine pastries.

While the pastries are proving, preheat the oven to 160°C fan/180°C/320°F/gas 4.

To make the salted caramel sauce, place the sugar and water in a saucepan over a medium heat until the sugar has dissolved and is starting to caramelize. Stir until smooth and a deep golden colour.

Remove from the heat and carefully whisk in the cream. It will steam and spit a little, so take care. Whisk in the butter and place back over a medium heat. Bring to the boil for 1 minute, whisking all the time. Remove from the heat and whisk in the fine salt. Place on one side to cool.

Brush the pastries with egg, and bake one tray at a time. Bake for 20–25 minutes until risen, golden and crisp.

Place on a wire rack to cool. Drizzle a little of the caramel sauce over each pastry (warm it gently if it's gone a little stiff). Finally, sprinkle a few sea salt flakes on each pastry.

Pains au chocolat

This is one of the best-loved breakfast pastries in Europe. A good pain au chocolat should have two cores of chocolate running through it. Any less and it's just not right. They are really easy to make. For a supply of breakfast pastries, as soon as you have shaped the pastries, pop them in the freezer in an airtight container. Pull a couple out of the freezer before you go to bed and they will defrost and prove overnight, ready to be baked for a delicious fresh breakfast in the morning.

MAKES 12 PASTRIES

Time required: 45 minutes preparation and one prove

Baking time: 20–25 minutes

Optimum oven position and setting: centre and no fan, with a baking stone

Essential equipment:
Two baking sheets; mine are aluminium and measure 38 x 32cm. Line with non-stick baking parchment
A couple of large bags to put the baking sheets into for proving
A disposable piping bag fitted with a 1mm plain round nozzle

INGREDIENTS
1 quantity of Danish pastry dough (page 175)
200g white chocolate
200g dark chocolate
1 medium egg, beaten, for glazing

To decorate
50g milk chocolate

METHOD
Cut the white and dark chocolate into 1cm wide strips and set aside.

Cut the cold block of Danish pastry in half. On a well-floured surface, roll out half of the pastry to a 42 x 20cm rectangle. With the long edge nearest you, lay a strip of the white chocolate right across the dough. Roll up the dough to just cover and encase the chocolate.

Next, place a strip of the dark chocolate right across the dough against the roll you just made. Roll up the dough like a Swiss roll. You should have two cores of chocolate running right through the roll.

Using a sharp knife, cut the dough into six equal pieces and place on a baking sheet. Place the baking sheet in a large bag and prove for 45 minutes at room temperature. Make sure the bag doesn't touch the dough.

Repeat for the second batch of dough to make 12 pastries in total.

While the pastries are proving, preheat the oven to 180°C fan/200°C/350°F/gas 6.

Brush the pastries with egg, and bake one tray at a time. Bake for 20–25 minutes until risen, golden and crisp.

Place on a wire rack to cool.

To decorate, melt the milk chocolate and place it in a piping bag fitted with a 1mm plain round nozzle. Drizzle over the pastries.

Nut & raisin vanilla turnovers

These are a really simple and quick to make Danish pastry and are a great version to experiment with different toppings. Try fresh or canned fruits, jams and nuts. You can even use ready-made custard for speed.

METHOD

First, make the custard. Put the milk and cream in a small saucepan over a low heat and bring to just below boiling point.

In a heatproof bowl, whisk together the egg yolks, sugar and vanilla until smooth and pale. Whisk in the cornflour until well combined. Pour the hot milk into the egg mixture in a slow steady stream, whisking all the time.

Place the mixture back in the saucepan over a low heat, stirring all the time until it thickens and coats the back of a spoon. You can cook it to perfection by using a temperature probe and heating the custard until it reaches 75°C/167°F. Be careful not to take it much higher than 80°C/176°F, or it will curdle. Pour it back in the bowl and place on one side to cool.

Cut the cold block of Danish pastry in half. On a well-floured surface, roll out half of the pastry to a 40cm square. Cut the square into nine smaller 10cm squares.

Place 2 teaspoons of the custard on two opposite corners of a pastry square. Place a walnut half on each teaspoon of custard and sprinkle some raisins and pistachios around each one. Pull over the two uncovered opposite corners and pinch together.

Repeat for the other eight squares of dough.

Place the baking sheet in a large bag and prove for 45 minutes at room temperature. Make sure the bag doesn't touch the dough.

Repeat for the second batch of dough so you end up with 18 pastries in total.

While the pastries are proving, preheat the oven to 180°C fan/200°C/350°F/gas 6.

Brush the pastries with egg and bake one tray at a time. Bake for 15–20 minutes until risen, golden and crisp.

Place on a wire rack to cool.

MAKES 18 PASTRIES

Time required: 45 minutes preparation and one prove

Baking time: 15–20 minutes

Optimum oven position and setting: centre and no fan, with a baking stone

Essential equipment:
Two baking sheets; mine are aluminium and measure 38 x 32cm. Line with non-stick baking parchment
A couple of large bags to put the baking sheets into for proving

INGREDIENTS
1 quantity of Danish pastry (page 175)
36 walnut halves
50g raisins
50g pistachio kernels
1 medium egg, beaten, for glazing

For the vanilla custard
150ml whole milk
50ml double cream
2 large egg yolks
40g caster sugar
½ tsp vanilla paste
1 tbsp cornflour

Choux pastry

Choux pastry is truly magical. How such a thick paste inflates to the lightest crisp pastry never ceases to amaze me. Here we have two versions of choux for you to try, sweet and chocolate. It's often said chocolate choux doesn't rise as well, but I can't really tell the difference.

There are a couple of things you can do to ensure success when making choux pastry. Firstly, the mixture should be thick and not too runny. It should just barely drop off a spatula when picked up. Secondly, when making éclairs, use a French star piping nozzle. The ridges it makes in the choux help the éclairs rise evenly. Check out my tip on how to pipe opposite.

Sweet choux pastry

**MAKES 12 ÉCLAIRS,
OR 35 MEDIUM-SIZE
PROFITEROLES**

Time required: 25 minutes preparation

Baking time: 35 minutes

**Optimum oven position
and setting:** centre and fan

Essential equipment:
A baking sheet; mine is
    aluminium and measures
    38 x 32cm
Non-stick baking parchment
A large disposable piping bag
    fitted with a 15mm French
    star nozzle
An electric hand or
    kitchen mixer

INGREDIENTS
150g plain flour
6 large eggs, beaten
110ml water
85ml whole milk
85g soft unsalted butter
1 tsp sunflower oil
¼ tsp fine salt
1½ tsp caster sugar

METHOD
Preheat the oven to 170°C fan/190°C/340°F/gas 5.

Put the flour in a bowl. Put the eggs in another bowl and beat lightly. Put the water, milk, butter, sunflower oil, salt and sugar in a large saucepan and bring to the boil. Remove from the heat and stir in the flour until well combined.

Place the pan back over a medium heat and cook for 2–3 minutes, stirring all the time with a spatula. Listen out for a crackling sound coming from the pan. This is a sign that the flour is cooked and ready. Remove from the heat and place in a large mixing bowl. Leave to cool for 10 minutes.

Using an electric or kitchen mixer, whisk the eggs into the mixture a little at a time until the mixture reaches a thick dropping consistency – you may not need all the eggs. The consistency is right when you lift out a large spoon of mixture and it takes a few seconds to drop off.

Place the mixture into the piping bag and set aside.

On a piece of non-stick baking parchment the same size as your baking sheet, mark 12 lines, each 15cm long, then turn it over so you can see the lines through the parchment. Dab some spots of the choux mixture on the four corners of the baking sheet and stick the parchment to it. Pipe 12 éclairs, using the lines as a guide. Using a wet finger, smooth any peaks on the éclairs.

Sprinkle the baking sheet with some water: this will create steam during baking, helping the choux rise. Bake for 35 minutes until well risen, golden and crisp.

Place on a wire rack to cool.

Chocolate choux pastry

METHOD
Follow the instructions for the sweet choux pastry opposite and simply combine the flour and cocoa powder together before adding to the liquid.

MAKES 12 ÉCLAIRS, OR 35 MEDIUM-SIZE PROFITEROLES

INGREDIENTS
110g plain flour
40g unsweetened
    cocoa powder
6 large eggs, beaten
110ml water
85ml whole milk
85g soft unsalted butter
1 tsp sunflower oil
¼ tsp fine salt
1½ tsp caster sugar

TIP

How to pipe choux pastry

Piping is daunting for many people when they start making choux pastry. Yes, it's true that practice makes perfect, but here are a couple of tips for success. Make sure that your choux pastry is not runny – you need a thick dropping consistency, so don't add too much egg – otherwise the piping bag will empty itself as soon as you pick it up and the choux will fall flat. The pastry should come out when you apply even pressure.

When piping, hold the tip of the nozzle about 1cm above your baking sheet. The contents need room to come out and form a shape. After you have piped your éclair or choux bun, stop the pressure and quickly lift the piping bag away to make a neat finish.

Strawberry cheesecake éclairs

These are a little different to the usual cream-filled éclairs. Strawberries and cream cheese, what's not to like? Make sure you use fondant icing sugar for the topping as it's much more stable than just regular icing sugar. Make sure it's really thick, too, so it doesn't run down the sides. It's worth investing in a 15mm wide flat piping nozzle to apply the fondant strip on the top of the éclair. Feel free to use a good-quality strawberry jam if you don't have time to make your own.

MAKES 12 ÉCLAIRS

Time required: 90 minutes preparation

Essential equipment:
A hand or kitchen mixer fitted
   with a whisk
Disposable piping bags,
   a 15mm flat piping nozzle,
   a large star nozzle and a
   1mm plain round nozzle

INGREDIENTS
1 quantity of 12 sweet
   choux éclairs (page 180)
strawberry jam (page 26),
   made with 150g fresh
   strawberries and
   1 tbsp lemon juice, or use
   100g shop-bought jam

For the cream cheese filling
300g full-fat soft
   cream cheese
225g icing sugar
finely grated zest of
   1 unwaxed lemon
300ml double cream

For the topping
300g fondant icing sugar
red food colouring gel

METHOD
Make a batch of 12 sweet choux éclairs (page 180).

Place the jam in a piping bag fitted with a 15mm flat piping nozzle.

To make the filling, put the cream cheese and icing sugar in a large mixing bowl and whisk until smooth. Add the lemon zest and double cream and whisk just until stiff. Be careful not to over-whisk it. Place it in a piping bag fitted with a large star nozzle.

Cut each éclair in half and pipe a line of jam in the base of each one. Next pipe a thick line of filling on the strawberry jam. Place the top on each éclair and press it down gently.

To make the topping, put the fondant icing sugar in a mixing bowl and add a little water until you have a really thick, smooth icing. Take 2 tablespoons of the icing and place in a piping bag fitted with a 1mm plain round nozzle.

Add a little red gel food colouring to the remaining icing to make a bright red colour. Place in a piping bag fitted with a 15mm flat piping nozzle. Pipe a single line of red fondant on the top of each éclair.

Pipe some strawberry shapes on the red fondant with the white fondant. Leave to set for 30 minutes.

Chocca mocca éclairs with candied walnuts

Coffee, chocolate and walnuts are a tried and tested flavour combination so it seemed only logical to try it in an éclair. These are not too sweet, so they're perfect for someone who usually steers away from this type of pastry.

MAKES 12 ÉCLAIRS

Time required: 90 minutes preparation

Essential equipment:
A hand whisk or a kitchen mixer fitted with a whisk
Disposable piping bags, a large star nozzle and a 15mm flat piping nozzle

INGREDIENTS
1 quantity of 12 chocolate choux éclairs (page 181)

For the coffee chocolate cream filling
1 tbsp instant coffee
50ml boiling water
300g mascarpone cheese
50g icing sugar
400ml double cream
50g dark chocolate, grated

For the candied walnuts
100ml water
100g caster sugar
36 walnut halves

For the chocolate fondant topping
25g unsweetened cocoa powder
25ml boiling water
400g fondant icing sugar

METHOD
Make a batch of 12 chocolate choux pastry éclairs (page 181).

To make the coffee chocolate cream, dissolve the coffee in the boiling water and set aside to cool.

Place the mascarpone, icing sugar and cooled coffee in a large mixing bowl and whisk until smooth. Add the cream and whisk until just stiff. Be careful not to over-whisk it. Fold in the grated chocolate until well distributed. Place it in a piping bag fitted with a large star nozzle.

Cut each éclair in half and pipe a thick line of filling on the base of each éclair.

Place the top on each éclair and press it down gently.

To make the candied nuts, place the water and caster sugar in a saucepan and bring to the boil. Tip in the nuts and simmer for 15 minutes. Lift out the nuts with a slotted spoon and place on a baking sheet lined with non-stick baking parchment to dry.

To make the topping, dissolve the cocoa powder in the boiling water. Put the fondant icing sugar in a mixing bowl and add the cocoa mixture. Mix well until you have a really thick, smooth icing. Add a little water if it is too thick, but if it is too thin it will run down the sides of the éclairs. Place the fondant in a piping bag fitted with a 15mm flat piping nozzle and pipe a line on the top of each éclair.

Place three walnuts on the top of each éclair and leave to set for 30 minutes.

Lemon meringue éclairs

I'm finishing my éclair journey influenced by lemon meringue pie. Look at it this way: the choux replaces the pastry and you end up with a perfect pick-up-and-eat treat. The filling is sharp and tangy, one for the lemon lovers, and each éclair is topped with a flamed Italian meringue. Go for it!

MAKES 12 ÉCLAIRS

Time required: 90 minutes preparation

Essential equipment:
A kitchen mixer fitted with a whisk
Disposable piping bags fitted with a large star nozzle
A kitchen blowtorch

INGREDIENTS

1 quantity of 12 sweet choux éclairs (page 180)

For the lemon curd cream filling
500ml double cream
5 tbsp icing sugar
2 tbsp limoncello liqueur
100g good-quality lemon curd (or make your own, page 27)

For the Italian meringue topping
3 medium egg whites (120g)
½ tsp cream of tartar
180g caster sugar
75ml water

METHOD

Make a batch of 12 sweet choux pastry éclairs (page 180).

To make the lemon curd cream, put the cream and icing sugar in a large mixing bowl and whisk until soft peaks form. Add the limoncello liqueur and whisk until just stiff. Gently fold in the lemon curd so the mixture is barely mixed and rippled. Place it in a piping bag fitted with a large star nozzle.

Cut each éclair in half and pipe a thick line of filling on the base of each éclair.

Place the top on each éclair and press it down gently.

Make the Italian meringue. Place the egg whites in a spotlessly clean kitchen mixer bowl and whisk until soft peaks form. Add the cream of tartar and whisk again briefly.

Put the sugar and water in a saucepan and place over a medium heat; stir until the sugar dissolves. Increase the heat to high and bring the syrup to just over 115°C/240°F, using a sugar thermometer. Start the mixer again at a medium speed and slowly trickle in the hot syrup. Increase the speed to full and whisk until the meringue becomes glossy, thick and is still just warm.

Immediately place in a piping bag fitted with a star nozzle and pipe a line of meringue on the top of each éclair. Toast the meringue gently with a blowtorch and serve within 2 hours.

Chouquettes

The chouquette is a bite-size ball of choux pastry, traditionally topped with a little nibbed sugar. In France, they are the go-to between-meals snack sold by the pâtisseries. Here are a couple of versions for you to try. I've injected some flavour into them with the use of a crumble that melts over the choux pastry during baking. The recipes share the same base ingredients, so you could try them both at the same time. If you want to stay traditional, just top the choux with nibbed sugar.

Matcha green tea chouquettes

MAKES ABOUT 30 CHOUQUETTES

Time required: 60 minutes preparation

Baking time: 20 minutes

Optimum oven position and setting: centre and fan

Essential equipment:
A baking sheet; mine is aluminium and measures 38 x 32cm
Non-stick baking parchment
An electric hand mixer and mini food processor
Disposable piping bag fitted with a 6mm plain round nozzle
A 2cm round cutter

INGREDIENTS

For the matcha green tea crumble
65g plain flour
1 tsp matcha green tea powder
75g caster sugar
65g cold unsalted butter

For the chouquettes
75g plain flour
1 tsp matcha green tea
3 large eggs, beaten
50ml water
50ml whole milk
40g soft unsalted butter
½ tsp sunflower oil
¼ tsp fine salt
½ tsp caster sugar
1 tbsp icing sugar
30g nibbed sugar

METHOD

Preheat the oven to 170°C fan/190°C/340°F/gas 5.

Make the matcha crumble first. Place all the ingredients in a small food processor and pulse until it resembles fine breadcrumbs. Tip it out into a bowl and, using your hands, form it into a dough.

Roll out the dough between two pieces of non-stick baking parchment to a thickness of about 2mm. Place on a baking sheet in the fridge while you make the chouquettes.

Put the flour and matcha tea in a bowl. Put the eggs in another bowl and beat lightly. Put the water, milk, butter, sunflower oil, salt and caster sugar in a large saucepan and bring to the boil. Remove from the heat and stir in the flour until well combined.

Place the pan back over a medium heat and cook for 2–3 minutes, stirring all the time with a spatula. Listen out for a crackling sound coming from the pan. This is a sign that the flour is cooked and ready. Remove from the heat and place in a large mixing bowl. Leave to cool for 10 minutes.

continues overleaf...

Using an electric or kitchen mixer, whisk the eggs into the mixture a little at a time until the mixture reaches a thick dropping consistency – you may not need all the eggs. The consistency is right when you lift out a large spoon of mixture and it takes a few seconds to drop off.

Place the mixture in a piping fitted with a 6mm plain round nozzle and set aside.

On a piece of non-stick baking parchment the same size as your baking sheet, draw 20 evenly spaced 2cm diameter circles, then turn it over so you can see the circles through the parchment.

Dab some spots of the choux mixture on the four corners of the baking sheet and stick the parchment to it. Pipe 30 chouquettes, using the circles as a guide to get them all the same. Using a wet finger, smooth any peaks on the chouquettes. Sift the icing sugar over the chouquettes.

Take the matcha crumble out of the fridge and carefully peel off the top sheet of parchment. Using a 2cm round cutter, cut out as many rounds as there are chouquettes. Peel the discs off the parchment and carefully place one on each chouquette. Sprinkle a few pieces of nibbed sugar on each disc.

Sprinkle the baking sheet with some water; this will create steam during baking, helping the choux rise. Bake for 20 minutes until well risen, golden and crisp.

Place on a wire rack to cool.

Chocolate hazelnut chouquettes

MAKES ABOUT 30 CHOUQUETTES

Time required: 60 minutes preparation

Baking time: 20 minutes

Optimum oven position and setting: centre and fan

Essential equipment:
A baking sheet; mine is aluminium and measures 38 x 32cm
Non-stick baking parchment
An electric hand mixer and mini food processor
Disposable piping bag fitted with a 6mm plain round nozzle
A 2cm round cutter

INGREDIENTS

For the chocolate crumble
65g plain flour
3 tsp unsweetened cocoa powder
75g caster sugar
65g cold unsalted butter

For the chouquettes
75g plain flour
3 large eggs, beaten
50ml water
50ml whole milk
40g soft unsalted butter
½ tsp sunflower oil
¼ tsp fine salt
½ tsp caster sugar
1 tbsp icing sugar
40g chopped roasted hazelnuts

METHOD
The method is exactly the same as for the matcha green tea chouqettes above.

The cocoa powder replaces the matcha green tea powder in the crumble.

The chopped hazelnuts replace the nibbed sugar for topping them off.

Chocolate heaven profiteroles

Here's one for the chocolate lovers. Profiteroles are so wonderfully retro yet never seem to go out of fashion. Serve these on a big platter with the sauce poured over them just before you present them to your guests. Trust me, they won't hang around for long.

METHOD

Ideally, make the chocolate crème pâtissière the day before and place in the fridge overnight.

Preheat the oven to 170°C fan/190°C/340°F/gas 5.

Put the flour in a bowl. Put the eggs in another bowl and beat lightly. Put the water, milk, butter, sunflower oil, salt and sugar in a large saucepan and bring to the boil. Remove from the heat and stir in the flour until well combined.

Place the pan back over a medium heat and cook for 2–3 minutes, stirring all the time with a spatula. Listen out for a crackling sound coming from the pan. This is a sign that the flour is cooked and ready. Remove from the heat and place in a large mixing bowl. Leave to cool for 10 minutes.

Using an electric or kitchen mixer, whisk the eggs into the mixture a little at a time until the mixture reaches a thick dropping consistency – you may not need all the eggs. The consistency is right when you lift out a large spoon of mixture and it takes a few seconds to drop off. Place the mixture in a piping bag fitted with a 12mm plain round nozzle and set aside.

On a piece of non-stick baking parchment the same size as your baking sheet, draw 20 evenly spaced 4cm diameter circles, then turn it over so you can see the circles through the parchment.

Dab some spots of the choux mixture on the four corners of the baking sheet and stick the parchment to it. Pipe 20 profiteroles, using the circles as a guide to get them all the same. Using a wet finger, smooth any peaks on the profiteroles.

Sprinkle the baking sheet with some water. This will create steam during baking, helping the choux rise. Bake for 25–30 minutes until well risen, golden and crisp.

Immediately you take them out of the oven, make a 5mm hole in the bottom of each choux ball with a knife and place on a wire rack to cool upside down. This lets the steam escape and keeps them crisp.

Take the chocolate crème pâtissière and give it a good whisk to loosen it. Place it in a piping bag fitted with a 4mm plain round nozzle and fill each profiterole through the steam vent hole. Place the profiteroles on your presentation place.

To make the chocolate sauce, place the dark chocolate and water in a heatproof bowl placed over a saucepan of simmering water. Make sure the water doesn't touch the bottom of the bowl. Stir until you have a smooth sauce. Pour over the profiteroles and coarsely grate the white chocolate over them all.

MAKES ABOUT 20 PROFITEROLES

Time required: 60 minutes preparation

Optimum oven position and setting: centre and fan

Essential equipment:
A baking sheet; mine is aluminium and measures 38 x 32cm
Non-stick baking parchment
An electric hand mixer
Disposable piping bags fitted with 12mm and 4mm plain round nozzles

INGREDIENTS
1 quantity (approx. 900g) of chocolate crème pâtissière (page 22)

For the profiteroles
75g plain flour
3 large eggs, beaten
50ml water
50ml whole milk
40g soft unsalted butter
½ tsp sunflower oil
¼ tsp fine salt
½ tsp caster sugar

For the chocolate sauce and topping
250g dark chocolate (70% cocoa solids)
180ml water
50g white chocolate

Gateau Saint Honoré

I couldn't write a book full of bakes without including the French dessert dedicated to the patron saint of bakers and pastry chefs, Saint Honoré. My version is simple to make, yet showstopping. Choux balls dipped in caramelized sugar and filled with Chantilly cream adorn the ring like giant pastry jewels. The centre is piped with even more cream and topped with summer fruits and glistening caramelized pecans.

SERVES 8

Time required: 2½ hours preparation

Baking time: about 1 hour

Essential equipment:
Two baking sheets; mine are aluminium and measure 38 x 32cm. Line with non-stick baking parchment
A few disposable piping bags, fitted with 4mm, 10mm, 12mm and large star nozzles
An electric hand or kitchen mixer
10 toothpicks

INGREDIENTS

a batch of sweet choux pastry (page 180)
250g ready-made puff pastry
10 pecan nut halves, with a toothpick gently pressed into each one
250g caster sugar
1 tbsp water
600ml double cream
6 tbsp icing sugar
2 tsp vanilla paste
15 fresh cherries with stalks
15 fresh strawberries
75g fresh blueberries
75g fresh raspberries

METHOD

Place the batch of sweet choux pastry in a piping bag with a 10mm plain round nozzle.

Preheat the oven to 200°C fan/220°C/390°F/gas 7. On a floured surface, roll out the puff pastry and cut out a 23cm diameter circle. Place on one of the lined baking sheets.

Pipe a ring of choux pastry on the inside edge of the puff pastry circle. Prick the exposed puff pastry all over with a fork. Bake for 10 minutes, then reduce the oven temperature to 180°C fan/200°C/350°F/gas 6, and bake for a further 20 minutes. Place on a wire rack to cool.

On a piece of non-stick baking parchment the same size as your baking sheet, draw 20 evenly spaced 4cm diameter circles, then turn it over so you can see the circles through the parchment. Dab some spots of the choux mixture on the four corners of the baking sheet and stick the parchment to it. Pipe 20 choux balls, using the circles as a guide to get them all the same. Using a wet finger, smooth any peaks on the choux.

Reduce the oven temperature to 170°C fan/190°C/340°F/gas 5. Sprinkle the baking sheet with some water – this will create steam during baking, helping the choux rise. Bake for 25–30 minutes until well risen, golden and crisp.

Immediately you take them out of the oven, make a 5mm hole in the bottom of each choux ball with a knife and place on a wire rack to cool upside down. This lets the steam escape and keeps them crisp.

To make the caramel, put the sugar and water in a saucepan over a medium heat until the sugar starts to dissolve and turn golden. Do not stir until it's virtually all dissolved. Once it's all smooth and golden, dip the bottom of the pan into some cold water. Working quickly, dip the top of each bun in the caramel and place on a lined baking sheet. Then dip each pecan nut into the caramel and place on the parchment.

Next make the vanilla cream. Place the cream, icing sugar and vanilla paste in a large mixing bowl and whisk until just stiff. Place a quarter of the cream in a piping bag fitted with a large star nozzle and pipe a ring of cream on top of the choux ring.

Place half of the remaining cream in a piping bag fitted with a 4mm plain round nozzle and fill each choux ball. This is easy to do as they should be tacked to the baking sheet by the caramel with the steam vent hole facing upwards.

Place the remaining cream in a piping bag fitted with a 10mm plain round nozzle and pipe short columns of cream in the centre of the puff pastry base, to cover it.

Place the choux buns on top of the cream on the choux ring. You will have some spares that can be served on the side. Fill the centre of the gateau with the fruit. Remove the toothpicks from the caramel-coated pecans and place them on top of the fruit.

CHAPTER 7
Honey

1. **Raspberry and honey salted shortbread**
A really easy shortbread cooking in a round tart tin. The dough is flavoured with freeze dried raspberries. Baked and then brushed with warm honey and sprinkled with sea salt flakes and baked again.

DECORATE BEFORE BAKING

2. **Honey fruit cake with cherry & almond bees**
A quick and easy round fruit cake with honey substituting for the sugar. Topped with almond and cherry bees.

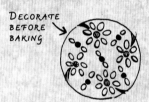

3. **Orange and honey drizzle cake**
The traditional lemon drizzle cake given a twist with orange and honey.

4. **Millionaire's shortbread**
A biscuit base with a honey caramel layer, topped off with a plain, milk and white chocolate marbled topping.

5. **Stockport honey buns**
A sweet bun filled with honey cream and topped with a fondant lemon daisy on the top.

HONEY
GLAZED

6. **Honey-glazed upside-down pineapple & cherry cake**
A twist on the old-fashioned upside-down pineapple cake with a honey glaze. The pineapple slices are cut into hexagons to resemble honeycomb.

7. **Honey-glazed pear tart**
A custard tart set with pears that have been caramalised in honey.

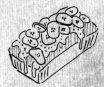

8. **Honey loaves**
Two recipes. First, a spiced tea and honey fruit loaf. Secondly a variation of the traditional banana loaf.

CRUMBLE
TOPPING

9. **Blueberry & honey muffins with an oat crumble**
Great breakfast blueberry muffins with an oat crumble, drizzled in honey.

Raspberry & honey salted shortbread

I guarantee you have never had shortbread like this before. It's crumbly with raspberry overtones and a salted, almost caramel-like chewy top. You need to make 16 slices, as 8 just aren't enough! The best thing of all is how easy it is to make.

MAKES 16 SLICES

Time required: 20 minutes preparation, plus chilling

Baking time: 45 minutes

Optimum oven position and setting: centre and fan

Essential equipment:
Two 23cm tart tins with loose bottoms; mine are 35mm deep. Grease and line the bottom of the tins with discs of non-stick baking parchment
A food processor fitted with a blade

INGREDIENTS
425g plain flour
150g caster sugar
3 tbsp cornflour
340g fridge-cold unsalted butter, cut into 2cm cubes
4 tbsp freeze-dried raspberries

For the salted honey glaze
50g runny honey
½ tsp coarse sea salt flakes

METHOD
Put the flour, sugar and cornflour in your food processor and give it a few quick pulses to mix it all up. Add the butter and pulse again until the mixture resembles fine breadcrumbs. Add the freeze-dried raspberries and give it a quick pulse to just mix them in.

Place one of your prepared tins on a set of scales and put just under half the mix into it. Do the same with the second tin and keep swapping them over until both tins contain half of the mix. Compact the mixture down evenly in each tin, using your fingers and palm of your hand. Place both tins in the fridge for 30 minutes.

Preheat the oven to 190°C fan/210°C/375°F/gas 6½.

Place both tins on the same oven shelf and bake for about 40 minutes until a deep golden colour. Remove from the oven.

Gently warm the honey in a microwave but don't boil it. Pour half of the honey over each of the shortbreads and spread it evenly using a pastry brush.

Sprinkle some sea salt flakes evenly over both shortbreads and place both back in the oven for about 4 minutes.

Remove from the oven and leave to cool in the tins for 10 minutes, then remove and place on a wire rack to cool completely.

Cut each shortbread into eight wedges. They will keep in an airtight container for 7 days.

Honey fruit cake with cherry & almond bees

I keep honeybees, and that is why honey makes so many appearances throughout my recipes. Totally natural, it's a great sweetener that adds a flavour all of its own. This is my version of a Genoa cake.

Honey replaces a huge amount of the sugar, giving a fantastic flavour running through the cake. Have some fun decorating the top with bees and flowers made from cherries and almonds.

SERVES 12

Time required: 45 minutes preparation

Baking time: 60–70 minutes

Optimum oven position and setting: below centre and fan

Essential equipment:
A 23cm non-stick springform cake tin, greased and lined with non-stick baking parchment

INGREDIENTS

250g soft unsalted butter
100g runny honey
100g light muscovado sugar
3 large eggs, beaten
250g self-raising flour
75g ground almonds
350g sultanas, lightly
   tossed in flour
50g dried apricots,
   coarsely chopped
50g candied chopped peel
finely grated zest of
   2 unwaxed lemons
1 tsp fine salt

To decorate

4 glacé morello cherries,
   cut in half
3 red glacé cherries, cut
   in half
50g blanched almonds
75g runny honey

METHOD

Preheat the oven to 160°C fan/180°C/320°F/gas 4.

Cream together the butter, honey and sugar until smooth and pale; this takes about 5 minutes in a kitchen mixer fitted with a paddle, or a little longer with a hand mixer.

Crack the eggs into a bowl and give them a quick mix. Slowly add them to the creamed mixture along with 1 tablespoon of the flour, beating all the time. Fold in the rest of the flour and the almonds until well mixed. Fold in the rest of the ingredients until just combined.

Pour the mixture into the prepared tin and smooth the top using a spatula or palette knife.

Decorate the top of the cake with the cherries and whole almonds. Use the morello cherries and two almonds to make bees and the red cherries with five almonds to make flowers.

Bake for 60–70 minutes. After 45 minutes, place a piece of foil loosely over the cake to stop the top getting too dark. After 60 minutes, check the cake: a skewer inserted into the centre should come out completely clean and the cake should feel firm to the touch. It may need longer.

When ready, leave the cake to cool in the tin for 15 minutes, then place on a wire rack to cool. While it is still warm, brush the top of the cake with the honey, to glaze.

Stockport honey buns

The Stockport honey bun is a thing of legend. They were a firm favourite among the residents of the town in the 1960s and 70s. However, as small independent bakeries began to close, so the honey bun began to disappear.

I remember eating the buns as a child. They were a real treat. You could really taste the honey. Reading around on local social media, Stockport residents still talk about the bun. So as a Stockport boy, born and bred, here's my homage to the legend.

MAKES 12 BUNS

Time required: 60 minutes preparation and two proves

Baking time: 10–12 minutes per batch

Optimum oven position and setting: centre and no fan, with a baking stone

Essential equipment:
Two baking sheets; mine are aluminium and measure 38 x 32cm. Line with non-stick baking parchment
A couple of large bags to put the baking sheets into for proving
A couple of disposable piping bags fitted with a filling nozzle and a 1mm plain round nozzle

INGREDIENTS
100ml milk
80ml boiling water
500g strong white bread flour
14g instant yeast
1 tsp salt
25g caster sugar
50g runny honey
35g soft unsalted butter
2 medium eggs
rapeseed oil for greasing

For the filling
350g double cream
100g runny honey

For the fondant topping
100g fondant icing sugar
yellow food colouring gel
½ tsp lemon extract
3–4 tsp lemon juice

METHOD

Put the milk in a heatproof jug and add the boiling water to give you a warm liquid. Put the flour, yeast, salt, sugar, honey, butter and eggs in a mixing bowl. When adding the yeast and salt, place them at opposite sides of the bowl. Add two-thirds of the liquid and begin to mix it all together with your fingers – or use a kitchen mixer with a dough hook. Add more liquid gradually until all the dry ingredients are picked up and you have a soft dough. You may not need all the liquid.

Tip the mixture out onto a clean surface and knead it for about 10 minutes. You will work through the initial wet stage and eventually end up with a smooth, soft, silky dough. If you are using a kitchen mixer, knead it for about 6 minutes.

Lightly oil a large bowl and place the dough in it. Cover it with clingfilm or a shower cap and leave it on one side until doubled in size. This dough will take about 2 hours to prove.

When the dough has proved, tip it onto a lightly floured surface. Knock it back slightly by folding it over itself several times. Weigh the dough and divide into 12 equal pieces.

Roll 6 pieces of dough into buns by making a cage shape with your hand and applying a gentle rolling pressure. As you roll them, place them on a prepared baking sheet. Space them apart so they don't touch.

Do the same with the remaining 6 on the other baking sheet. Place each baking sheet inside a large bag to prove. Make sure the bag doesn't touch the dough. Prove again for about another hour until doubled in size.

While the rolls are proving, preheat the oven to 180°C fan/200°C/350°F/gas 6.

When the buns have doubled in size, bake each tray separately for 10–12 minutes until golden. Place the buns on a wire rack to cool.

To make the filling, put the cream and honey in a large bowl and whisk until just stiff. Put the cream into the piping bag fitted with a filling nozzle.

Make a hole in the side of each bun, using a thin knife to pierce into the centre. Pipe 30g of filling into each bun. To achieve this, weigh each bun and then fill it, weighing it as necessary until it is 30g heavier.

To make the topping, put the fondant icing sugar in a bowl with a little food colouring and the lemon extract. Add a little lemon juice until you have a really thick smooth paste. Don't add too much lemon juice or it will become too runny. If that happens, add a little more fondant icing sugar to thicken it up again. Place the fondant in a piping bag fitted with a 1mm plain round nozzle and pipe a daisy design on the top of each bun.

Honey-glazed upside-down pineapple & cherry cake

Here's a great twist on the classic pineapple upside-down cake. The pineapple slices are cut into honeycomb shapes and black cherries represent a bee in the centre of each one. Well, you have to have fun sometimes! The honey self-glazes the cake when it's turned out and gives it an amazing flavour.

SERVES 6–8

Time required: 30 minutes preparation

Baking time: 35–45 minutes

Optimum oven position and setting: below centre and fan

Essential equipment:
A 20 x 30cm rectangular tin; I use a traybake tin, 5cm deep, with a loose bottom. Grease and line the tin with non-stick baking parchment.
A 7cm (at its widest point) hexagon cutter
A large disposable piping bag

INGREDIENTS
250g runny honey
15 canned pineapple slices (about 4 x 200g cans), drained
15 black morello glacé cherries
280g soft unsalted butter
280g golden caster sugar
3 large eggs, beaten
50g sour cream
1 tsp vanilla paste
4 tbsp milk
280g self-raising flour

METHOD
Preheat the oven to 170°C fan/190°C/340°F/gas 5.

Warm the honey in a small saucepan over a low heat or in a bowl in the microwave. Don't boil it. Pour it into the bottom of the prepared tin and move it around to create an even layer.

Cut the pineapple slices into hexagons, using the cutter. To do this, place a slice on a cutting board, rest the cutter on it and cut the excess pineapple away with a sharp knife. Place them in the bottom of the tin to resemble honeycomb. Place a cherry in the centre of each ring.

Cream together the butter and sugar until pale and fluffy; this takes about 5 minutes in a kitchen mixer fitted with a paddle, or a little longer with a hand mixer.

Crack the eggs into a bowl, add the sour cream and give them a quick mix. Slowly add them to the creamed mixture along with 1 tablespoon of the flour and the vanilla paste, beating all the time. Place the mixture in a large piping bag and pipe it evenly over the pineapples. Gently smooth it out with a spatula and make a slight well in the centre.

Place the baking tin on a baking sheet, just in case any of the honey leaks out, and bake for 35–45 minutes. After 35 minutes, check the cake: a skewer inserted into the centre should come out completely clean and the cake should feel firm to the touch and have shrunk away from the sides. It may need longer.

When ready, leave the cake to cool in the tin for 5 minutes.

Put your presentation plate on top of the tin and, in one swift move, turn it over and remove the tin. Serve warm or cold, with a scoop of vanilla ice cream.

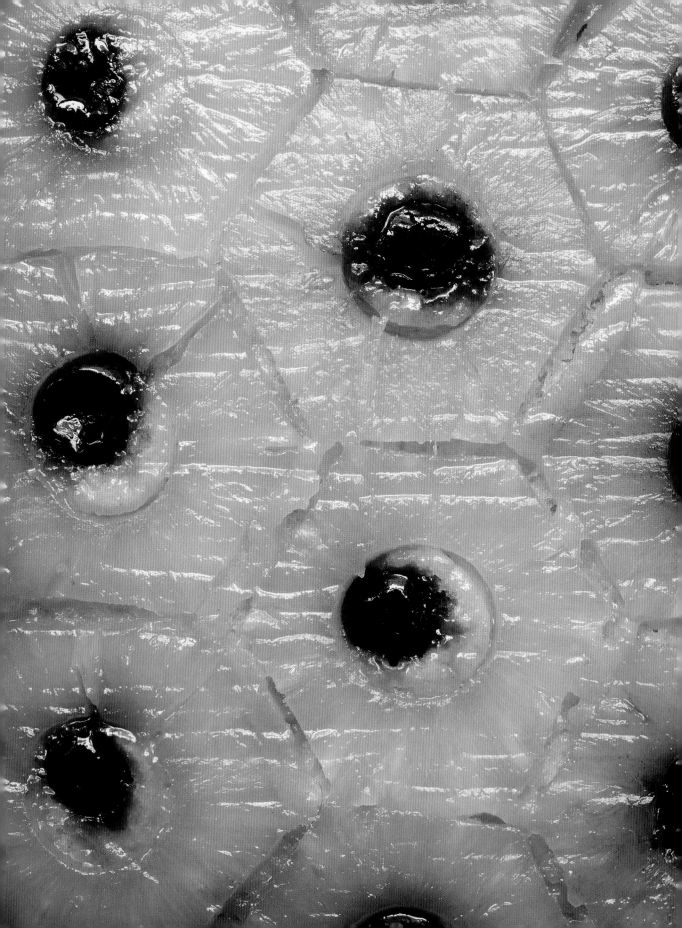

Honey-glazed pear tart

This is a real showstopper of a tart: it looks amazing, and the flavours are truly memorable; it's a firm family favourite. It takes a little time to prepare but it's totally worth it. Don't use pears that are too ripe: they will soften during the poaching and baking process. Serve it with a little whipped cream for that extra indulgence.

SERVES 12

Time required: 75 minutes preparation

Baking time: 30–35 minutes

Optimum oven position and setting: centre and fan

Essential equipment:
A 26cm tart tin with a
    loose bottom; mine is
    30mm deep
A baking sheet; mine is
    aluminium and measures
    38 x 32cm
A temperature probe

INGREDIENTS
1 quantity of sweet shortcrust
    pastry (page 15), blind
    baked in a 26cm tart tin

For the honey-glazed pears
5 semi-ripe Conference
    pears, peeled, quartered
    and cored
25g unsalted butter
3 tbsp runny honey
175ml smooth fresh
    orange juice

For the baked custard
4 medium eggs
finely grated zest of 2 oranges
finely grated zest of
    1 unwaxed lemon
130ml smooth fresh orange
    juice
160g caster sugar
1 tbsp rum
100ml double cream

METHOD
Preheat the oven to 130°C fan/150°C/ 270°F/gas 2.

Put the pears, butter, honey and orange juice into a large non-stick frying pan and bring to the boil. Reduce the heat slightly and simmer until the liquid has just evaporated and the pears are glazed. Remove from the heat and leave to cool.

To make the custard, crack the eggs into a large mixing bowl. Add the orange and lemon zest and the caster sugar. Stir gently until well combined, but don't get too much air into the mixture. Add the orange juice, rum and cream and stir gently until well mixed.

Transfer the mixture to a saucepan and very gently heat it to 50°C/120°F. Alternatively, place the mixture in a heatproof jug and warm it in a microwave on low, stirring it every 30 seconds. Doing this gives the custard a head start on setting in the oven and means your pastry case won't over-bake.

Arrange the quartered pears around the pastry case with the rounded outsides facing upwards. Depending on the size of your pears, you may not need them all.

Place the pastry case on a baking sheet on the oven shelf and gently pour the custard filling into the pastry case until about 3mm from the top. Take care not to spill any on the outside of the pastry as that would make it stick to the tart tin.

Bake for 30–35 minutes until just set, with a wobble in the centre. You can test if the tart is baked to perfection by using a temperature probe: the centre should be just over 75°C/165°F.

Place on a wire rack and leave to cool completely before removing the tart from the tin. Once completely cooled, place in the fridge until required.

Honey spiced tea loaf

The use of tea in baking is simply delightful. This is a somewhat old-fashioned recipe, thought to originate in Yorkshire, and it's a shame that it's becoming forgotten. The strong, fragrant tea is used to plump up the fruit overnight before baking. Go to the extra trouble of using Lady Grey tea when making this loaf: it really makes a difference. Butter a slice and enjoy with a cuppa. If you are feeling slightly more daring, though, my niece Zara tested this recipe for me and said a slice goes brilliantly with some mature Cheddar and a dash of chutney.

SERVES 10

Time required: 30 minutes preparation, plus overnight soaking

Baking time: 60–75 minutes

Optimum oven position and setting: below centre and fan

Essential equipment:
A 900g/2lb loaf tin; the base of mine measures 95 x 195mm and the tin is 70mm high. Grease and line it with non-stick baking parchment (see tip, page 39).

INGREDIENTS

2 Lady Grey tea bags
175ml boiling water
100g runny honey
100g raisins
200g sultanas
50g dried cranberries
1 large egg, beaten
1 tsp mixed spice
225g self-raising flour

For the glaze
25g runny honey

METHOD

The night before you want to make the loaf, place the teabags in a large heatproof bowl. Pour the boiling water over the teabags and leave to brew for 5 minutes before removing the teabags. Add the honey and dried fruits to the liquid and give them a good stir. Cover with clingfilm and leave on one side until the next day.

Preheat the oven to 160°C fan/180°C/320°F/gas 4.

Add the egg to the fruit mixture and stir well. Sift in the spice and flour and give it a really good stir until well mixed. Spoon the mixture into the prepared tin and level the top.

Bake for 60–75 minutes. After 35–40 minutes, cover the top of the loaf loosely with foil to stop it browning too much. After 60 minutes, check the cake: a skewer inserted into the centre should come out completely clean. It may need longer.

Remove from the oven when ready and leave to cool in the tin for 10 minutes, then turn out onto a wire rack. While the loaf is still warm, brush the top with the honey to glaze.

Tropical banana & honey bread

Banana bread is the go-to bake for many people and it never loses its popularity. My version is a little blinged-up. I find banana bread sometimes lacks a little bite, so I put some desiccated coconut in mine, along with a hint of pineapple and rum to just take things up a notch.

METHOD

Preheat the oven to 160°C fan/180°C/320°F/gas 4.

Cream together the butter and sugar until pale and fluffy; this takes about 5 minutes in a kitchen mixer fitted with a paddle, or a little longer with a hand mixer.

Slowly add the eggs to the creamed mixture along with 1 tablespoon of the flour, mixing all the time until incorporated. Add the rest of the ingredients and beat them in. Don't overwork the mixture, just make sure it's all well mixed. Spoon the mixture into the prepared tin and level the top.

Bake for 45–55 minutes. Cover the top of the loaf loosely with foil after 40 minutes if it is browning too much. After 45 minutes, check the cake: a skewer inserted into the centre should come out completely clean. It may need longer.

Remove from the oven when ready and leave to cool in the tin for 10 minutes, then turn out onto a wire rack to cool completely.

Make the lime icing. Place the icing sugar in a small bowl and gradually add lime juice until you have a thick smooth icing. Spoon it generously over the loaf. Sprinkle the banana chips and desiccated coconut on top.

SERVES 10

Time required: 30 minutes preparation

Baking time: 45–55 minutes

Optimum oven position and setting: centre and fan

Essential equipment:
A 900g/2lb loaf tin; the base of mine measures 95 x 195mm and the tin is 70mm high. Grease and line it with non-stick baking parchment (see tip, page 39).

INGREDIENTS

75g soft unsalted butter
40g caster sugar
2 large eggs, beaten
225g self-raising flour
60g runny honey
2 ripe bananas, mashed
50g puréed pineapple chunks
finely grated zest of 1 lime
½ tsp baking powder
1 tbsp dark rum
1 tsp vanilla extract
½ tsp fine salt
25g desiccated coconut

For the topping
60g icing sugar
juice of ½ lime
½ tbsp coconut flakes
2 tbsp dried banana chips

Blueberry & honey muffins with an oat crumble

These are a great breakfast muffin that will easily keep for a couple of days in an airtight container. It's really worth making the crumble as it adds another dimension. However, it's not a deal-breaker and the muffins are perfectly delicious and succulent without it.

MAKES 12

Time required: 45 minutes preparation

Baking time: 20–25 minutes

Optimum oven position and setting: below centre and fan

Essential equipment:
A 12-hole muffin tin and 12 greaseproof paper muffin cases. The muffin cases I use have a bottom diameter of 50mm, top diameter of 80mm and are 44mm high. You could also use tulip muffin cases.

INGREDIENTS

3 medium eggs
75ml corn oil
50g runny honey
100g golden caster sugar
250ml buttermilk
1 tsp vanilla paste
350g self-raising flour
½ tsp baking powder
finely grated zest of
    1 unwaxed lemon
225g fresh blueberries

For the crumble

25g cold unsalted butter, cut
    into 1cm cubes
25g plain flour
½ tsp ground cinnamon
30g demerara sugar
25g rolled oats

For the drizzle

3 tsp runny honey

METHOD

Preheat the oven to 200°C fan/220°C/390°F/gas 7. Place a muffin case in each hole of your muffin tin.

Make the crumble first. Put the butter in a mixing bowl with the flour and cinnamon, and rub with your fingers until it resembles fine breadcrumbs. Briefly rub in the sugar and oats until well combined. Set aside.

In a bowl, whisk together the eggs, corn oil, honey and sugar until smooth and pale. Whisk in the buttermilk and vanilla paste until well mixed. Sift in the flour and baking powder. Add the lemon zest and stir until just combined.

Next, I put the cake mixture into a disposable piping bag, cut the end off the piping bag and evenly pipe a small amount of the mixture into each muffin case. The piping bag allows perfect control and makes it much easier to put an equal amount of mixture in each case, rather than using a spoon or ice-cream scoop.

Divide the blueberries among the muffin cases. Pipe the remaining mixture evenly into each case, covering the blueberries.

Sprinkle the crumble evenly among the 12 muffins, filling to the top of the cases.

Bake for about 20–25 minutes until the tops are firm and a skewer inserted in the centre of a muffin comes out clean.

Remove the muffins from the oven, take them out of the tin and immediately place them on a wire rack to cool.

When the muffins are cool, drizzle a little honey over the top of each one.

CHAPTER 8
Taste of Spain

1. Roscos de anis
My mum's aniseed-flavoured doughnuts. Totally unique.

2. Cortadillos
My grandfather's sweet bite-size pastries drowned in honey.

PERFECT FOR DUNKING!

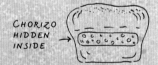

CHOCOLATE SAUCE →

3. Cinnamon churros with dark chocolate dipping sauce
Traditional churros with a spicy twist.

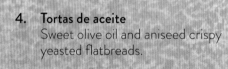

OLIVE OIL AND ANISEED →

4. Tortas de aceite
Sweet olive oil and aniseed crispy yeasted flatbreads.

CHORIZO HIDDEN INSIDE →

CROSS OF ST JAMES →

5. Tarta de Santiago
A traditional Spanish almond tart with chestnuts.

6. **Mantecados**
    Traditional Spanish shortbreads made from lard.

7. **Bizcochos de soletilla con pistachio**
    Pistachio sponge fingers, ideal for dunking.

8. **Empanadas**
    Spiced minced beef and chickpea empanadas made with a citrus pastry.

9. **Chorizo loaf**
    A traditional loaf with a cured spicy chorizo running through the centre of it.

10. **Roscon de reyes**
    Sweet and savoury versions of the iconic Spanish Epiphany centrepiece breads. The sweet version is an orange-flavoured enriched dough baked with colourful glacé fruits on the top. The savoury version is filled with olives, peppers, jamón de Serrano and Manchego cheese, and decorated with olives and a white flour paste.

7. **Olive curon**
    An intertwined wreath loaf packed with olives.

11. **Paella**
    OK, so I know this isn't a baking recipe, but so many people ask me how to make a good paella, I need to include it!

Roscos de anis – Aniseed doughnuts

If there is one recipe that sums up my childhood and earliest memories, it's these Spanish doughnuts. This is a really old family recipe. It was passed to my mum by her auntie and she remembers these from her childhood. I've lost count of the number of times I've been asked for the recipe for these. So here it is.

When I was a child, the day my mum was making these was almost ceremonial. The ingredients were out, the large mixing bowl (which she has now passed down to me), the frying pan with hot aniseed-flavoured oil filling the house with its aroma. These doughnuts are like nothing else I have ever tasted. They are quite biscuity, light and crisp and are amazing with a cup of tea or coffee. When mum showed me the recipe, the quantity of sugar used was measured in eggshell halves, which I thought was wonderful. I think it's a shame how many recipes must have been lost in time that have not been handed down through the generations.

For real authenticity, you should use an aniseed-flavoured liqueur from Spain. I use Anis del Mono Dulce. It's tricky to get hold of in the UK but it can be found. If you are struggling to find it, use another aniseed-flavoured liqueur such as Sambuca or Pernod.

You will also need aniseeds to make the aniseed-infused olive oil: these are easily sourced online. I usually make a large batch of this oil in advance and keep it in a bottle for future use.

There are quite a few processes in the making of these doughnuts, but I'm not going to apologize as they are more than worth it. I usually make these the day before I want them as they are much better over the following few days. They easily last up to 4 days in an airtight container.

MAKES ABOUT 20 ROSCOS

Time required: 90 minutes

Frying time:
about 40–45 minutes

Essential equipment:
These doughnuts are deep fried, so a good electric deep fat fryer is essential for consistency and safety. I use sunflower oil for frying.
The dough is much easier to make in a kitchen mixer fitted with a paddle.
Two large baking sheets, well dusted with plain flour

INGREDIENTS

For the aniseed-infused olive oil

600ml extra-virgin olive oil
6 tbsp aniseeds

For the roscos

3 medium eggs
380g plain flour, plus extra for dusting
130g caster sugar
125ml aniseed-infused extra-virgin olive oil
7g baking powder
60ml aniseed liqueur

For coating

200g caster sugar

METHOD

Make the aniseed-infused olive oil. You can make this well in advance. Put the oil in a large saucepan with the aniseeds and place over a medium heat. Heat until the aniseeds turn a deep brown colour and you can smell the aroma of the spice. This takes about 5–8 minutes. You don't want to heat it for too long or you could burn the seeds. Leave to cool completely, then pass it through a fine sieve into a large jug. I then store it in a clean airtight bottle until I need it. It will keep for many months.

Flour your baking sheets really well to stop the doughnuts sticking to them while you shape them.

Place all the roscos ingredients in your mixer bowl and mix until well incorporated. The dough should be thick and sticky.

Preheat your deep fat fryer to 190°C/375°F.

continues overleaf...

Flour your hands really well and take a piece of dough about the size of a ping-pong ball. Working quickly, roll it into a ball then push a finger through it to form a ring doughnut about 8cm in diameter. Place it on a well-floured baking sheet. Continue until you have used all the dough. The doughnuts will begin to puff up slightly while you make them.

Once you have shaped them all, line some wire cooling racks with kitchen paper.

Begin frying the doughnuts in the order you made them. You will notice they have inflated and grown. Using a thin, floured fish slice or spatula, carefully lift up each doughnut and place it in the fryer – you don't want to lose the air the baking powder has created inside the doughnuts. I usually fry three at a time.

When you drop them into the fryer, leave them for about 30 seconds and then flip them over. Fry them for about 3 minutes on each side until a deep golden colour. They will really expand in the fryer.

Using a metal slotted spoon, lift them out and place them on the kitchen paper to drain and cool.

Once they have cooled slightly, coat them completely in caster sugar, shaking off the excess. Place them in an airtight container lined with kitchen paper, but don't put the lid on until completely cooled.

These will keep in an airtight container for up to 4 days.

Cortadillos

Another old family recipe passed on to me by mum. She tells me the story of how her father used to make them in the bar he owned in Spain. They would sell as quickly as he could make them. Best eaten fresh, I suppose they are almost a form of street finger food. They are such a neat bite-size sweet snack, almost like a fried mini doughnut but a bit more biscuity, each coated in sticky honey. You really should give them a go.

METHOD

Preheat your deep fat fryer to 190°C/375°F.

Place the flour, sugar and baking powder in a mixing bowl and give them a stir. Add the olive oil and orange juice, and start to mix with your hands, bringing all the ingredients together into a dough.

Tip the dough onto your work surface and knead it for about 3 minutes until smooth and elastic. Wrap in clingfilm for 5 minutes.

To make the honey coating, put the honey and boiling water into a bowl and stir until combined.

Divide the dough into three equal pieces. Roll each piece into a long sausage shape about 1cm thick. Cut the sausage into 2cm pieces.

Place all the pieces into the fryer for 6 minutes. While they are frying, roll and cut the next batch.

When golden brown and crisp, drain the cortadillos and immediately put them into the honey coating. Give them a good stir to coat and then place straight onto your presentation plate. Repeat until you have used up all the dough.

Drizzle a little extra honey over all the cortadillos and eat while hot.

MAKES ABOUT 60 BITE-SIZED CORTADILLOS

Time required: 25 minutes

Frying time: about 25 minutes

Essential equipment: Cortadillos need to be fried at a specific temperature, so a good electric deep fat fryer is essential for consistency and safety. I use sunflower oil for frying.

INGREDIENTS

200g plain flour
1 tbsp caster sugar
½ tsp baking powder
40ml extra-virgin olive oil
100ml smooth fresh orange juice

Honey coating

100g runny honey, warmed, plus extra for drizzling
2 tsp boiling water

Cinnamon churros with dark chocolate dipping sauce

As a child, I spent most summers at my grandmother's house in a town called Algeciras in southern Spain. Some mornings my mum and grandmother would go out to the market early and take me with them. The churros sellers would be out in force with their white carts, providing a satisfying breakfast on the go to passers by. The carts had a glass cabinet filled with freshly fried large churros spirals. They were served warm in a paper bag with some sugar thrown in. By 10am, the churros sellers had vanished for the day and I remember my disappointment if we were a little late and had missed them. Now with this recipe I can have them any time of the day!

MAKES ABOUT 30 CHURROS

Time required: 45 minutes

Frying time: about 30 minutes

Essential equipment:
The churros need to be fried at a specific temperature, so a good electric deep fat fryer is essential for consistency and safety. I use sunflower oil for frying.
A couple of large disposable piping bags
A large star nozzle
A couple of baking sheets lined with non-stick baking parchment

INGREDIENTS
300g '00' white flour
1½ tsp baking powder
½ tsp fine salt
2 tsp ground cinnamon
½ tsp mixed spice
400ml boiling water
2 tbsp extra-virgin olive oil
100g caster sugar for coating

For the chocolate dipping sauce
125ml double cream
100g dark chocolate
25g unsalted butter
1 tbsp runny honey

METHOD
Make the chocolate sauce first. Put all the ingredients in a saucepan and stir continuously over a low heat until the chocolate melts and you have a thick, glossy sauce. Pour into a clean bowl and set aside.

To make the churros, put the flour, salt, baking powder, cinnamon and mixed spice in a large heatproof bowl. Make a well in the centre.

Boil the water and add the olive oil. Pour the liquid into the well in the flour mixture and mix it for a minute or so with a wooden spoon until a dough starts to form. Tip it out onto a clean surface and knead for a minute once it has cooled slightly.

Preheat your deep fat fryer to 170°C/340°F.

Take a couple of large disposable piping bags and place one inside the other for strength. Fit a large star nozzle, then place the dough inside. Start squeezing the dough out onto the lined baking sheets in about 10cm lengths until you have used it all up.

Fry the churros in the deep fat fryer, three at a time, for about 90 seconds on each side.

Take them out using a slotted spoon and place them on kitchen paper to drain. While still warm, give them a good coating of caster sugar. Enjoy them as they are or by dipping them in the chocolate sauce.

Tortas de aceite (olive oil biscuits)

A really old traditional Spanish delicacy, which is said to be of Arab origin. The torta de aceite is a crisp and flaky sweet round biscuit. They are leavened using yeast, which gives them an incredible lightness. Flavoured with extra-virgin olive oil and aniseed, these biscuits are simply amazing. A few of them wrapped in greaseproof paper make a perfect gift.

MAKES ABOUT 20 TORTAS

Time required: 60 minutes preparation and one prove

Baking time: 5–6 minutes per batch

Optimum oven position and setting: centre and fan

Essential equipment:
Four baking sheets; mine are aluminium and measure 38 x 32cm. Line with non-stick baking parchment

INGREDIENTS
530g '00' white flour
3 tbsp caster sugar
1 tbsp aniseeds
3 tsp sesame seeds
1 tsp orange essence
10g instant yeast
1 tsp fine salt
190ml extra-virgin olive oil, plus extra for greasing and rolling out
2 tbsp aniseed liqueur (I use Anis del Mono Dulce, but Pernod or sambuca are fine)
170ml cool water

For dusting
100g caster sugar

METHOD
Place all the ingredients except the water into a large bowl. Add two-thirds of the water and begin to mix it all together with your fingers – or use a kitchen mixer with a dough hook. Add more water gradually until all the dry ingredients are picked up and you have a soft dough. You may not need all of the water.

Tip the mixture out onto a clean surface and knead it for about 10 minutes. You will work through the initial wet stage and eventually end up with a smooth, soft, silky dough. If you are using a kitchen mixer, knead it for about 8 minutes.

Lightly oil a large bowl and place the dough in it. Cover it with clingfilm or a shower cap and leave it on one side until doubled in size. Depending on your room temperature, this can take 1 hour, but it's fine to leave it for 2 hours. It will take slightly longer to prove than other doughs, due to the high olive oil content.

While the dough is proving, preheat the oven to 200°C fan/220°C/390°F/gas 7.

When the dough has proved, tip it onto an oiled surface and use your scales to divide it into 36g balls.

Using an oiled rolling pin, roll out each ball into a thin disc about 14cm in diameter and place them on the prepared baking sheets.

Sprinkle each torta with caster sugar and as soon as you have a full tray, place it immediately into the hot oven for 5–6 minutes until golden and crisp. Don't leave them in the oven too long as you don't want the sugar to burn.

Place on wire racks as soon as they come out of the oven. You can get a bit of a production line going here. As some are baking, roll out and prepare the next batch.

These will keep in an airtight container for up to a week.

Tarta de Santiago (St James cake)

This is a round almond cake that originated in Galicia, north-west Spain, in the Middle Ages. The top of the cake has an imprint of the cross of Saint James (*cruz de Santiago*), made by masking the shape and dusting liberally with icing sugar.

My version is incredibly moist, with strong citrus overtones, and is fantastic as a dessert. A hidden pastry base is coated with a layer of chestnut and vanilla spread and quartered chestnuts are hidden in the almond filling.

SERVES 10

Time required: 40 minutes

Baking time: 30–35 minutes

Optimum oven position and setting: centre and fan

Essential equipment:
A 23cm non-stick springform cake tin, greased and lined with non-stick baking parchment
Make a cardboard template, cutting out the shape of the cross of St James (see template on page 253).

INGREDIENTS

1 quantity of sweet shortcrust pastry (page 15), or 250g ready-made sweet pastry
140g chestnut and vanilla spread
4 medium eggs
160g golden caster sugar
finely grated zest of 2 oranges
finely grated zest of 2 unwaxed lemons
160g ground almonds
½ tsp ground cinnamon
1 tbsp sherry or 1 tsp vanilla extract
200g cooked, peeled and ready to use whole chestnuts, quartered
25g icing sugar

METHOD

Roll out the pastry to about 3mm thick. Using the cake tin as a template, cut out a circle of pastry and place it in the bottom of the prepared tin.

Spread the chestnut spread over the pastry base, but don't go right to the edge – leave about 1cm free. Place in the fridge while you make the filling.

Preheat the oven to 170°C fan/190°C/340°F/gas 5.

Whisk the eggs and sugar together for about 5 minutes until the whisk leaves a thick trail when lifted out.

Fold in the orange zest, lemon zest, ground almonds, cinnamon and sherry until well mixed. Finally, fold in the chopped chestnuts and pour the mixture into the cake tin. Spread it out gently and evenly using a spatula.

Bake for 30–35 minutes until golden and the centre feels firm.

Leave to cool in the tin for 10 minutes, then release from the tin and place on a wire rack to cool completely.

Place the cardboard template on top of the cake and dust liberally with icing sugar; very carefully lift off the template before serving.

Mantecados (Spanish shortbreads)

The Christmas treats package sent from my grandmother every year during my childhood would always include a couple of boxes of *mantecados* (or *polvorones* as they are also known at Christmas). Inevitably the boxes would only last a few days, as the delicious contents were not available in the UK at the time. Even now, many years later, they haven't really hit our stores, which is rather surprising because they go perfectly with a cup of tea. They really are still one of Spain's greatest secrets.

It's hard to describe them, but in essence they are a form of shortbread. Exceptionally crumbly and traditionally wrapped in tissue paper to catch the crumbs as you tuck in – a few of them encased in different coloured wrappers make the perfect Christmas gift.

MAKES ABOUT 30 MANTECADOS

Time required: 30 minutes preparation

Baking time: 30 minutes per batch

Optimum oven position and setting: centre and fan

Essential equipment:
Two baking sheets; mine are aluminium and measure 38 x 32cm. Line with non-stick baking parchment
A 5cm round cutter

INGREDIENTS

350g strong white bread flour
175g lard, softened
140g caster sugar
2 tbsp cream sherry
½ tsp ground cinnamon
80g ground almonds
2 tbsp sesame seeds
50g icing sugar for dusting

METHOD

Place the flour in a large frying pan over a medium heat. Stir continuously until just toasted and taking on some colour. Place in a large mixing bowl to cool.

Preheat the oven to 150°C fan/170°C/300°F/gas 4.

Cream together the lard and sugar until pale and fluffy; this takes about 5 minutes in a kitchen mixer fitted with a paddle, or a little longer with a hand mixer.

Add the sherry and cinnamon to the lard mixture and mix again until well mixed. Add the flour and ground almonds and mix well. The mixture will be very dry and crumbly.

Tip it out onto your work surface and compact it down flat, using your hands, to a thickness of about 1.5cm. Cut out 5cm rounds and gently place them on the prepared baking sheets. Sprinkle a few sesame seeds on the top of each mantecado.

Bake the mantecados one tray at a time for 30 minutes until they are a deep golden colour and look dry.

Leave to cool on the baking sheets as they are extremely fragile while hot.

When completely cool, dust with icing sugar.

Bizcochos de soletilla con pistachio (pistachio sponge fingers)

If there's one thing I realized early on in my life it's that Spanish people like to dunk treats into tea and coffee. I have fond memories of sitting at the kitchen table in my grandmother's house in Spain for afternoon tea. We would eat buttered fresh bread with jamón or chorizo and mini sponge cakes. Everything was dunked, regardless of whether it was sweet or savoury! It's in my DNA and I carry on the tradition to this day. Here is my recipe for some really light and crisp sponge fingers. Feel free to leave the pistachio paste out, but it's worth putting it in for a fragrant after-taste and delicate bite. These are sturdy enough to be dunked into your favourite cuppa, but also make a perfect substitute for ladyfingers in a trifle or tiramisu.

MAKES ABOUT 30

Time required: 20 minutes preparation

Baking time: 20 minutes, plus cooling

Optimum oven position and setting: centre and fan

Essential equipment:
A baking sheet; mine is aluminium and measures 38 x 32cm.
Non-stick baking parchment
A disposable piping bag fitted with a 1.5cm plain round nozzle

INGREDIENTS

50g plain flour
40g cornflour
3 medium eggs, separated
65g caster sugar
1 tsp vanilla paste
25g pistachio nut paste
2 tbsp icing sugar

METHOD

Preheat the oven to 180°C fan/200°C/360°F/gas 6.

On a piece of non-stick baking parchment the same size as your baking sheet, mark lines 8cm long, spaced 1cm apart, then turn it over so you can see the lines through the parchment. Line your baking tray with the parchment.

Mix together the plain flour and cornflour in a bowl and set aside.

In a spotlessly clean bowl, whisk the egg whites until soft peaks form, then gradually whisk in 40g of the caster sugar until thick and glossy. Set aside.

Add the remaining sugar to the egg yolks and whisk until pale and fluffy. Add the vanilla paste and pistachio nut paste to the egg yolk mixture and whisk briefly until incorporated and smooth.

Pour the egg yolk mixture into the egg whites and fold gently, using a large metal spoon, until just incorporated.

Next, sift in the flour mixture into the mixture in 3 batches, folding in each time until just mixed. Do this gently so as not to lose too much of the air.

Place the mixture in a piping bag fitted with a 1.5cm plain round nozzle and pipe fingers onto the prepared parchment using the lines you drew earlier as a guide. Make sure you leave about 1cm space between them. Sprinkle the fingers liberally with icing sugar using a sieve.

Bake for 20 minutes until well risen, golden and crisp. They are ready when they come away cleanly from the parchment.

Place on a wire rack to cool. These will keep in an airtight container for up to 4 days.

Empanadas

Every year as a child in the 1970s and 1980s I spent the entire summer in Spain. I remember big family meals and my dad taking me to small local bars that served tapas. Empanadas were a staple bar snack and here, many years later, is my take on them. They are deep fried and filled with a delicious spiced minced beef. Waxy charlotte potatoes and chickpeas give the filling a satisfying bite. Great hot or cold, they are the perfect snack, especially with a beer or glass of tinto!

MAKES 12 EMPANADAS

Time required: 90 minutes

Frying time: about 40–45 minutes

Essential equipment:
These empanadas are deep fried, so a good electric deep fat fryer is essential for consistency and safety. I use sunflower oil for frying.
The pastry is much easier to make in a food processor fitted with a blade.
Two baking sheets, greased with a little rapeseed oil
I use a 15cm cutter to cut out the pastry rounds, but you could also cut around a small plate.

INGREDIENTS
For the pastry
375g plain flour, plus extra for dusting
¼ tsp fine salt
1 tsp baking powder
115g cold unsalted butter
2 tsp sweet (*dulce*) smoked paprika
finely grated zest of 1 unwaxed lemon
160ml ice-cold water

For the filling
150g charlotte potatoes, peeled and cut into 8mm cubes
2 tbsp olive oil
1 small red onion, finely chopped
2 garlic cloves, finely chopped
200g raw cooking chorizo, cut into 5mm cubes
75g smoked pancetta
375g lean minced beef
1 beef stock cube
2 tsp dried oregano
1 tsp dried parsley
1 tsp cumin seeds
2 tsp sweet (*dulce*) smoked paprika
½ tsp chilli flakes
pinch of cayenne pepper
1 red pepper, seeded and finely diced
140g drained canned chickpeas
2 tbsp tomato purée
4 tbsp water
fine salt and freshly ground black pepper

METHOD
Boil the potatoes in salted water for about 6 minutes until just tender. Drain and place in a bowl of cold water to stop them cooking.

To make the pastry, place all the ingredients except the water in a food processor and pulse until the mixture resembles fine breadcrumbs. Slowly add the water, mixing continuously, until a ball of dough forms. Tip out onto a clean work surface and knead until smooth. Divide in two and wrap in clingfilm. Place in the fridge while you make the filling.

Place a large non-stick deep frying pan or wok over a medium heat and pour the olive oil into it. Add the onion, garlic, chorizo and pancetta, and fry for a few minutes. Add the minced beef, stock cube, herbs and spices, and fry until browned.

Add the red pepper and chickpeas to the pan along with the tomato purée and water, and cook for another 5 minutes. Taste and check for seasoning; add salt and pepper as required. Remove from the heat, add the cold potatoes and stir through. Check the seasoning again and spread out the mixture in a clean roasting tin to cool quickly.

Flour your work surface well. Roll out one half of the pastry to about 2mm thick. Cut out six 15cm rounds and place each one on a plate with a piece of clingfilm between each one. Cover with clingfilm and place back in the fridge.

Repeat with the other half of the pastry and place in the fridge.

continues overleaf...

When the filling has completely cooled, take out the first batch of pastry rounds from the fridge.

Preheat the deep fat fryer to 180°C/360°F. Grease a baking sheet with a little rapeseed oil.

Take one round of pastry in your hand. Using a finger, brush some water around the edge. Place about 2 tablespoons of the filling in the centre, then fold over and press the edges together. Crimp the edges to seal: I pinch and twist to make a rope shape, but you can simply use the tines of a fork to seal each parcel. Place the pastry on the greased baking sheet and prepare another.

Place both pastries in the deep fat fryer and fry for 3–4 minutes on each side, turning regularly, until deep golden brown and puffed up.

Remove from the fryer using a slotted spoon and drain on kitchen paper.

While they are frying, prepare the next two and get a production line going until you have made 12 empanadas. Can be eaten hot or cold.

Chorizo loaf

I love the way chorizo has been so happily adopted in the British diet. As a child, I would eagerly await the food package sent from Spain, as it always contained a whole chorizo sausage – unknown in the UK back in the 1970s. Nowadays, visit any supermarket and not only do you have chorizo, but many kinds and flavours. With our passion for sausages and spicy food, the chorizo is the perfect combination to satisfy those needs. It's so versatile too. Slapped between two pieces of bread it makes a delicious sandwich. When cooked, it releases its fat and flavours and lifts a dish to new heights. I've gone down the route of combining chorizo and bread. It's my earliest memory of eating chorizo and it's still my most enjoyable way of eating it today.

MAKES 1 LOAF

Time required: 30 minutes preparation and two proves

Baking time:
30–40 minutes

Optimum oven position and setting: centre and no fan, with a baking stone

Essential equipment:
A 900g/2lb loaf tin; the base of mine measures 95 x 195mm and the tin is 70mm high. Grease and line it with non-stick baking parchment.
A large bag to put the loaf tin into for proving

INGREDIENTS

250g strong white bread flour, plus extra for dusting
250g strong wholemeal bread flour
10g instant yeast
1 tsp fine salt
½ tsp freshly ground black pepper
320ml cool water
a little rapeseed oil for greasing the proving bowl
225g Spanish cured ring chorizo – you will need 18cm of chorizo

METHOD

Place both flours, the yeast, salt and pepper in a large bowl. When adding the yeast and salt, place them at opposite sides of the bowl.

Add two-thirds of the water and begin to mix it all together with your fingers - or use a kitchen mixer with a dough hook. Add the rest of the water gradually until all the dry ingredients are picked up and you have a soft dough. You may not need all of the water.

Tip the mixture out onto a clean surface and knead it for about 10 minutes. You will work through the initial wet stage and eventually end up with a smooth, soft, silky dough. If you are using a kitchen mixer, knead it for about 6 minutes.

Lightly oil a large bowl and place the dough in it. Cover it with clingfilm or a shower cap and leave it on one side until doubled in size. Depending on your room temperature, this can take 1 hour, but it's fine to leave it for 2 hours.

When the dough has proved, tip it out onto a lightly floured surface (I use rice flour). Fold it over on itself a couple of times to knock it back.

Roll the dough out to a 15 x 25cm rectangle with the longest edge nearest you. Place the chorizo in the centre of the long edge nearest you and then roll it up tightly like a Swiss roll, to encase the chorizo sausage.

With the seam at the bottom, tuck the two ends of the dough underneath itself and place in the prepared loaf tin.

Place the tin in a large bag and prove again until the dough is level with the top of the tin. Make sure the bag doesn't touch the dough.

While the loaf is proving, preheat the oven to 200°C fan/220°C/390°F/gas 7.

When the loaf has risen, dust the top with a little flour, using a fine sieve.

Bake for 15 minutes, then reduce the oven temperature to 170°C fan/190°C/340°F/gas 5, and bake for a further 30 minutes. It should have a deep golden colour and sound hollow when tapped. You can test if it is baked to perfection by using a temperature probe: the centre of the loaf should be just over 90°C/195°F.

Place on a wire rack to cool.

Roscon de reyes

A traditional Spanish sweet bread, usually eaten to celebrate Epiphany on 6 January, the *roscon de reyes* is heavily decorated, to celebrate the arrival of the three kings visiting the infant Jesus. The translation of the name is 'the kings' ring' and the bread is usually round or oval. A trinket in the shape of a figure is usually hidden in the dough before baking, along with a dried butter bean. It is said that whoever finds the figure is crowned 'king' or 'queen' of the celebration, whereas whoever finds the bean has to pay for the following year's Epiphany party.

If you search online, there are some fantastic glacé fruits you can buy to decorate the bread. I use glacé orange slices, different coloured cherries and angelica, as well as whole blanched almonds and a sprinkling of nibbed sugar. All glacé fruits will survive the heat of the baking process perfectly.

I'm also going to break with tradition and show you a savoury version. Both of these breads are fantastic at any time of year, great for sharing, and will command pride of place on any table. Let your artistic side run wild when decorating, and put your personal stamp on them.

SERVES 12

Time required: 45 minutes and two proves

Baking time: 30–35 minutes

Optimum oven position and setting: centre and no fan, with a baking stone

Essential equipment:
A baking sheet; mine is aluminium and measures 38 x 32cm. Line with non-stick baking parchment
A large bag to put the baking sheet into for proving

INGREDIENTS FOR SWEET ROSCON DE REYES

90ml whole milk
50g soft unsalted butter
25ml cold water
350g strong white bread flour
10g instant yeast
½ tsp fine salt
75g caster sugar
1 medium egg, plus 1 egg, beaten, for glazing
finely grated zest of 1 orange
1 tbsp rum
a little rapeseed oil for greasing the proving bowl

To decorate
Your choice of candied fruits and zests, glacé cherries, nibbed sugar, figs, whole almonds or other whole nuts

METHOD

Warm the milk and butter together until the butter has just melted. Then add the water and stir to mix.

Place the flour, yeast, salt, sugar, 1 egg, orange zest and rum in a large bowl. When adding the yeast and salt, place them at opposite sides of the bowl.

Add two-thirds of the liquid and begin to mix it all together with your fingers – or use a kitchen mixer with a dough hook. Add the rest of the water gradually until all the dry ingredients are picked up and you have a soft dough. You may not need all of the liquid.

Tip the mixture out onto a clean surface and knead it for about 10 minutes. You will work through the initial wet stage and eventually end up with a smooth, soft, silky dough. If you are using a kitchen mixer, knead it for about 6 minutes.

Lightly oil a large bowl and place the dough in it. Cover it with clingfilm or a shower cap and leave it on one side until doubled in size. Depending on your room temperature, this can take 2 hours, but it's fine to leave it for 3 hours.

continues overleaf...

When the dough has proved, tip it out onto a lightly floured surface and knock it back gently by folding it over itself a couple of times. Form it into a ball and then, using your fingers, make a hole in the middle. Keep your hands well floured and gradually make a large ring shape about 28cm in diameter. The centre hole should be about 11cm in diameter. If you are hiding trinkets in the bread, use a sharp knife to make holes in the sides and insert them, then press the holes closed. Place the bread on the lined baking sheet and pop it in a large bag to prove for about an hour until doubled in size. Make sure the bag doesn't touch the dough.

Preheat the oven to 160°C fan/180°C/320°F/gas 4.

Brush the proved ring gently with the beaten egg. Lightly place your choice of decorations on the top and sides of the dough ring; they will stick to the egg glaze and there is no need to press them down, or you risk deflating your dough.

Bake for 30–35 minutes until a deep golden colour. You can test if the bread is baked to perfection by using a temperature probe: the centre should be just over 90°C/195°F.

Leave to cool on a wire rack before enjoying. Best eaten on the day of baking.

Savoury roscon de reyes

Here is my recipe for a savoury roscon de reyes. I love this bread – a slice is like a sandwich full of my favourite things. It's decorated with olives and a flour paste is used to draw a pattern on the top, a bit like the cross on hot cross buns. Kept in an airtight container in a cool place, it will last a couple of days...not that it ever hangs around that long. However, it really is at its best on the day it is baked, so why not invite some friends and family over and make both of these breads to treat them.

The key to success with this bread is to make sure the olives and peppers used in the filling are dried really well using kitchen paper. Moisture inside the bread will make it soggy and give you some big gaps.

METHOD

First make the dough. Place all the ingredients in a large bowl, except the water. When adding the yeast and salt, place them at opposite sides of the bowl.

Add two-thirds of the water and begin to mix it all together with your fingers – or use a kitchen mixer with a dough hook. Add the rest of the water gradually until all the dry ingredients are picked up and you have a soft dough. You may not need all of the water.

Tip the mixture out onto a clean surface and knead it for about 10 minutes. You will work through the initial wet stage and eventually end up with a smooth, soft, silky dough. If you are using a kitchen mixer, knead it for about 6 minutes.

Lightly oil a large bowl and place the dough in it. Cover it with clingfilm or a shower cap and leave it on one side until doubled in size. Depending on your room temperature, this can take 1 hour, but it's fine to leave it for 2 hours.

When the dough has proved, tip it out onto a lightly floured surface (I use rice flour). Use and knock it back gently by folding it over itself a couple of times.

Give the surface another dusting of flour and roll out the dough to a 52 x 20cm rectangle with a long side nearest you. Starting with the long side nearest to you, place the ham on the dough in two long strips. Place the red pepper strips on the ham, followed by the Manchego cheese. Sprinkle the chopped olives evenly all over the dough,

continues overleaf...

SERVES 12

Time required: 60 minutes and two proves

Baking time: about 35 minutes

Optimum oven position and setting: centre and no fan, with a baking stone

Essential equipment:
A baking sheet; mine is aluminium and measures 38 x 32cm. Line with non-stick baking parchment
A large bag to put the baking sheet into for proving
A disposable piping bag fitted with a 2mm plain round nozzle

INGREDIENTS

500g strong white bread flour
10g instant yeast
10g fine salt
15g caster sugar
1 tbsp extra-virgin olive oil
1 tsp sweet (*dulce*) smoked paprika
300ml cool water
a little rapeseed oil for greasing the proving bowl

For the filling

100g thinly sliced Spanish serrano ham, torn into strips
140g roasted red pepper (ready-to-use, in oil or brine), cut into 1cm wide strips, dried well on kitchen paper
100g Manchego cheese, cut into 3mm thick strips
160g pitted black or green olives, coarsely chopped and dried well on kitchen paper
coarsely ground black pepper

ingredients continue overleaf

To decorate

20 pepper-stuffed
   green olives
20 pitted black olives
2 or 3 roasted red peppers
   (ready-to-use, in oil or
   brine), cut into eight strips,
   1cm wide and about 10cm,
   dried well on kitchen paper
50g plain flour
3 tbsp water
1 medium egg, beaten,
   for glazing

followed by a good twist of black pepper – leave about 3cm of the long side furthest away from you filling free, as that will seal the whole roll together.

If you are hiding trinkets in the bread, place them on the filling on the long side nearest you. Starting at one long side, roll up the dough tightly into a giant Swiss roll.

Place it on your prepared baking sheet and bring both ends of the roll around to each other to form a perfect round ring. Neatly tuck one inside the other and press them together firmly to join.

Using a sharp pair of scissors, cut four slots about 2cm deep, evenly spaced apart, in the outside of the ring. Next, cut another four slots, evenly spaced between the first four, so you end up with eight cuts. Finally, cut another slot between each of the eight, so you end up with 16 in total. These slots will let steam escape from inside the loaf and will look fantastic.

Place the baking sheet inside a large bag to prove. Make sure the bag doesn't touch the dough. Prove for 45 minutes.

While the loaf is proving, preheat the oven to 160°C fan/180°C/320°F/gas 4.

Prepare the decoration items. Cut all the olives neatly in half and slice the peppers. Mix the flour and water together to form a stiff paste and place in a piping bag fitted with a 2mm plain round nozzle.

Remove the loaf from the proving bag and brush gently with the beaten egg. Gently place the olives and peppers on and around the sides of the roscon. Pipe a design around them with the flour paste.

Bake for about 35 minutes until a deep golden colour. You can test if the loaf is baked to perfection by using a temperature probe: the centre should be just over 90°C/195°F.

Leave to cool on a wire rack before enjoying. Can be eaten warm or cold.

Variation
STUFFED PICNIC MUFFINS

This recipe lends itself brilliantly to making 12 stuffed muffins, which are great for a picnic or packed lunches. Place 12 tulip muffin cases into a 12-hole muffin tin.

Follow the recipe right up until you have rolled the dough like a Swiss roll.

Cut your dough into 12 equal pieces. Place each piece with the spiral facing upwards in a muffin case. Place the muffin tin inside a large bag and prove for an hour.

Preheat the oven to 160°C fan/180°C/320°F/gas 4.

Bake for 25 minutes until golden. You can test if the muffins are baked to perfection by using a temperature probe: the centre of one of them should be just over 90°C/195°F.

Drizzle the top of each one with some extra-virgin olive oil. Can be eaten hot or cold.

Index

Pumpkin pie template

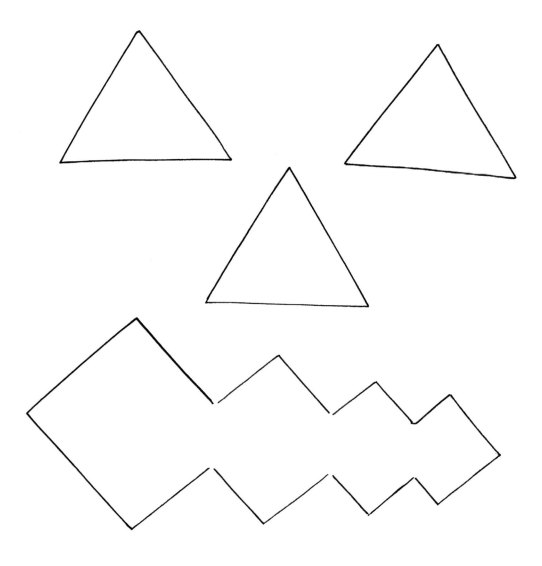

For use with recipe on page 149.

Tarta de Santiago template

For use with recipe on page 226.

Conversion charts

The recipes in this book were devised and tested using metric measurements. Any conversion from metric will introduce a possibility of error and may make your finished result less successful. However, not everyone is happy to use metric so I have provided these conversion charts to assist you. These are approximate conversions, which have either been rounded up or down. Never mix metric and imperial measures in one recipe; stick to one system or the other.

NOTE ABOUT VOLUME MEASUREMENTS
American cups do not convert automatically from metric – a cup of caster sugar weighs more than a cup of flour, for instance. For accurate cup conversions refer to the USDA resource as it will give more reliable conversions based on the density of the food stuff in question. Or try: www.foodinfo.us/densities.aspx

Weights

grams	ounces
25	1
50	2
75	3
110	4
150	5
175	6
200	7
225	8
250	9
275	10
315	11
350	12
365	13
400	14
425	15
450	1 lb

Volumes

ml	fl oz
5	1 teaspoon
15	½ or 1 tablespoon
25	1
55	2
75	3
120	4
150	5
175	6
200	7
225	8
250	9
275	10
425	15
570	1 pint
725	1¼ pints
850	1½ pints
1 litre	1¾ pints

Dimensions

Imperial	Metric
⅛ inch	3 mm
¼ inch	5 mm
½ inch	1 cm
¾ inch	2 cm
1 inch	2.5 cm
1¼ inch	3 cm
1½ inch	4 cm
1¾ inch	4.5 cm
2 inch	5 cm
2½ inch	6 cm
3 inch	7.5 cm
3½ inch	9 cm
4 inch	10 cm
5 inch	13 cm
5¼ inch	13.5 cm
6 inch	15 cm
6½ inch	16 cm
7 inch	18 cm
7½ inch	19 cm
8 inch	20 cm
9 inch	23 cm
9½ inch	24 cm
10 inch	25.5 cm
11 inch	28 cm
12 inch	30 cm

Where to buy equipment & ingredients

When coming up with the recipes in this book, my main aim was to keep them all accessible with regards to equipment and ingredients. Virtually everything should be available in your local shops and supermarkets. However, here are a few stores and suppliers where I shop to get certain items.

Tins, muffin cases, pipettes, equipment and consumables

Lakeland
www.lakeland.co.uk

Amazon
www.amazon.co.uk

Aluminium baking sheets

Silverwood Bakeware
www.alansilverwood.co.uk

Temperature probe

Thermapen
www.thermapen.co.uk

Aniseeds and other spices

Healthy Supplies
www.healthysupplies.co.uk

Glacé fruits

Buy Wholefoods Online
www.buywholefoodsonline.co.uk

First published in the United Kingdom in 2015 by
Pavilion
1 Gower Street
London
WC1E 6HD

ISBN: 978-1-91049-644-2

A CIP catalogue record for this book is available
from the British Library.

10 9 8 7 6 5 4 3 2 1

Reproduction by Rival Colour UK
Printed and bound by 1010 Printing International Ltd., China

This book can be ordered direct from the publisher at
www.pavilionbooks.com

Commissioning Editor: Emily Preece-Morrison
Photographer: Clare Winfield
Design Concept and Cover: Laura Russell

Publisher's acknowledgements:
Thanks are also due to Maggie Ramsay, Wei Tang, Maud Eden,
Allan Somerville and Vanessa Bird.